BREAD
FIRE *and*
WATER

BREAD
FIRE *and*
WATER

*The Laws of Niddah
within the Jewish Marriage*

*The Laws of Lighting Candles
for Shabbat and Yom Tov*

*The Laws of Separating
Challah from Dough*

FELDHEIM PUBLISHERS

JERUSALEM   NEW YORK

Warmest thanks to all those who have assisted us in the publishing of this book. Special appreciation to D. Gast, Z. & T. Hammond, F. Klipstein, Rabbi Y. Levinberg, R. Rechnitzer, Rabbi S. Rosenbaum and Rabbi R. Simon for their valuable contributions.

Original text in German: 'Die reine jüdische Ehe' by Auriel Silbiger, Basle, Switzerland

English translation: 'Bread, Fire and Water' by S. Cymerman, London, England

French translation: 'Vivre le Mariage avec la Tora' by A. Weil, Strasbourg , France

ISBN 1-58330-467-3

Cover photo by Prisma Dia-Agentur, Zürich

FELDHEIM PUBLISHERS
POB 35002 / Jerusalem, Israel

202 Airport Executive Park
Nanuet, NY 10954

www.feldheim.com

Printed in Israel

Rabbi CHAIM P. SCHEINBERG

KIRYAT MATTERSDORF
PANIM MEIROT 2
JERUSALEM, ISRAEL

הרב חיים פנחס שיינברג
ראש ישיבת תורה אור
ומורה הוראה דקרית מטרסדורף
ירושלים

בס"ד

מכתב תהילה

The author of this book has in the past published several sefarim on Halacha, highly recommended by Gedolei Yisrael. He is especially to be commended for his practical guide to the halachot of taharat hamishpachah (family purity) and other subjects particularly affecting the Jewish housewife, in which he has endeavored to present the practical application of these complex laws (הלכות) in a concise and clear manner.

This new English translation will help to strengthen the meticulous observance of taharat hamishpachah, an issue so vital to the spiritual survival of the Jewish people. Its clear and unambiguous form will be an aid to those already observing these laws, and we hope will also encourage wider circles to practice them.

Wishing the author success in his spreading of Torah observance.

Rabbi Chaim Pinchus Scheinberg
Adar I 5760

Author's Preface

Bread, fire, and water – three basic elements in human existence. Since God wanted His blessing (ברכה) to abide within these materials, he awarded us with mitzvot in connection with each of them: *challah* for bread, Shabbat and Yom Tov candles for fire, and *mikveh* for water.

Every Jew must observe these three mitzvot, which hold a special ability to create an atmosphere of Judaism in the home. The main merit of keeping these mitzvot, however, was entrusted to the woman, the housewife (see *Mishnah Shabbat* 2:6). We find in the story of Sarah, that she was blessed in these three things: the cloud which remained over her tent (a sign of *taharah*, purity), the blessing in her dough (*challah*), and her light which burned from one *Erev Shabbat* to the next (Gur Arieh, *Chayei Sarah* 24:67). We also find that in Hannah the prophetess' prayer to God to take pity on her and grant her a child, she mentions specifically these mitzvot, which she kept with special precision. Her prayers were answered, and she gave birth to Samuel (*Berachot* 31b). An acronym has been given to these commandments, which spells out Hannah's name in Hebrew:

חנה: **ח**לה, **נ**דה, **ה**דלקת הנר

A summary of the laws concerning these mitzvot has been gathered in this book to enable each and every one to study them, especially brides and grooms about to embark on the building of a new home.

Through keeping these mitzvot, may we all merit Jewish homes specially blessed by God.

Contents

THE LAWS OF SEPARATING
CHALLAH FROM DOUGH

The Laws of Niddah

Introduction to the Laws of Niddah

The Torah contains 613 mitzvot, every one of which is an integral part of the overall Divine plan for the nourishment of the soul and the enrichment of the lives of the Jewish people. In some cases, the benefits or necessity of a particular mitzvah are manifest, as in the case of honoring parents and the prohibition against slander, and in other cases, less so. Some mitzvot, those known as *chukkim* (חוקים – statutes), are generally beyond human comprehension. We follow these laws without actually understanding the reason behind them but simply because God, our Creator, commanded us to do so. Some of these laws, such as the prohibition of eating pork, are upheld by many Jews, whereas others, such as the laws of *niddah*, are widely neglected nowadays, largely due to ignorance of their importance.

In fact, the laws of *niddah*, often referred to as *taharat hamishpachah* (Family Purity), rank as one of the fundamental precepts of our religion, alongside Shabbat and *brit milah*. The Jewish family is the bedrock on and around which the rest of the Jewish faith is built, and its purity has, therefore, been paramount throughout the ages. Even in times of severe hardship and during periods of persecution, Jewish women have always persevered to observe this mitzvah, often to the point of self-sacrifice.

The term *niddah* means distanced, i.e. separated from one's husband. It describes the status of a woman, from the moment blood flows from her uterus, usually at the start of her monthly period, until the moment she immerses herself in a kosher *mikveh* (מקוה – ritual bath) at the right time. The Biblical source for this is the verse in Leviticus (18:19): "Do not come close to a woman who is ritually unclean due to her menstruation." This verse prescribes the law of complete abstinence between a couple while the woman is a *niddah*.

Despite our inability to fully understand the reasons and rationale behind these laws, we are, nevertheless, often able to perceive the beneficial effects and resultant advantages of keeping the rules of *taharat hamishpachah*.

Every couple aspires to have a successful, loving, and exciting marriage. This is not easily achieved and is even more difficult to maintain. With the passage of time, marriage becomes routine, lacks novelty and, generally, the feeling of growing and developing together wanes. It is no secret that, throughout the western world, the institution of marriage is under severe strain. Who does not have friends, acquaintances, or even family members who have lived through the tragedy of a failed or unhappy marriage? While offering no panaceas and instant solutions for the complex problems which are ever present in a marriage, the discipline of *taharat hamishpachah* usually eases the tensions that may permeate a marriage and often injects the spark of excitement and the magic which is often absent. As husband and wife must abstain from all physical contact, even the merest touch, during the *niddah* period, they will experience a feeling of renewal and romance when they are re-united each month. This leads to a deeper and more satisfying relationship which will be based on love, understanding, and respect (*Talmud Niddah* 31b). Many married couples who start keeping these laws after several years of married life speak enthusiastically of the transformation that their relationship undergoes and of the renewed vitality of their marriage.

The laws of *niddah* also provide an added advantage from a medical perspective. During menstruation, the mucus in the vagina turns from being acidic to alkaline and, in addition, the plug of mucus, which normally blocks the opening of the cervix, is washed away. These two changes render the vagina vulnerable to infection from the outside. It has been found that, consequently, abstaining from intercourse during menstruation substantially decreases the possibility of infection.

The aim of this short book is to acquaint the reader with the practical details of the laws of *niddah* and how they interact with daily life. The chapters that follow offer a readable, concise, and comprehensive guide to the laws of *taharat hamishpachah*, as well as a brief treatment of the two additional mitzvot that are traditionally the special province of the Jewish woman, lighting the candles for Shabbat and Yom Tov and the separation of *challah* from dough.

May the study and observance of these mitzvot serve to strengthen the bond between husband and wife, as well as between the People of Israel and their Creator.

I
In a Nutshell

A brief outline of the laws of niddah is presented in this chapter. This will enable the reader, when studying the detailed chapters of the book, to appreciate how a particular section of law relates to, and is a part of, the whole picture.

Becoming a *niddah*

A woman becomes a *niddah* from the moment that blood leaves her uterus. Usually, this occurs at the onset of menstruation but can occur at other times too. (See Chapter 5.)

During the time of *niddah*

While a woman has a status of a *niddah*, marital relations, physical contact, and other forms of intimacy are not allowed. (See Chapter 6.)

Leaving the state of *niddah*

The status of *niddah* ceases only when all the following stages have been successfully completed:

☐ She must verify that her menstrual bleeding has ceased completely. This is known as a *hefsek taharah*. (See Chapter 2.)

☐ A period of seven consecutive spotless days, without any bleeding, follows next. These days are called the *seven clean days*. (See Chapter 3.)

☐ In the evening after the "seven clean days" have ended, the woman immerses herself in a *mikveh* (ritual bath). After the immersion, termed *tevilah*, the status of *niddah* ends. Marital relations, physical contact, and other forms of intimacy are again permitted. (See Chapter 4.)

Expecting the onset of the next period

To avoid an inadvertent transgression of the laws of *niddah*, a woman must calculate the anticipated onset of her next period in advance. At that time marital relations are not allowed. (See Chapter 7.)

The *bedikah* (בדיקה – examination)

It is reasonably possible for a tiny drop of blood to leave the womb and remain in the vagina, without being noticed. Therefore, a woman must, at certain times, make an internal examination of her vagina – known as a *bedikah* (plural, *bedikot*) – using a *bedikah*-cloth, to determine whether this has, in fact, occurred.

In the following chapters, we will learn under which circumstances a woman is obliged to make a *bedikah*. The method of making a *bedikah* will be described in Chapter 3, p. 14.

2
The Hefsek Taharah
(הפסק טהרה)

A woman is able to immerse in a mikveh only after seven consecutive days, during which she must be free from any bleeding. Towards dusk before the start of her "seven clean days," a woman must verify, by making a bedikah, that her menstrual bleeding has ceased completely. This bedikah, together with the laws pertaining to it, is known as hefsek taharah. Only by performing the hefsek taharah can a woman establish that her menstruation has ceased. The "seven clean days" start from the day after a successful hefsek taharah has been achieved.

1. When is hefsek taharah performed?

The earliest time at which a woman performs *hefsek taharah* is on the fifth day after she has become a *niddah*. This applies even if her bleeding ceases before the fifth day.

Day One starts at the commencement of bleeding and ends at nightfall. Thus, if bleeding commences a few minutes before nightfall, Day One will last for only those few minutes and Day Two will start immediately thereafter. If, however, bleeding starts just after nightfall, then Day Two will start after the following nightfall (when a new Jewish day begins).

Working Example

*If a woman becomes a niddah after nightfall on Tuesday evening or during the day of Wednesday itself, then Wednesday is considered the first of her five days. She can then perform hefsek taharah towards dusk on Sunday afternoon, **only if** her bleeding has ceased completely by then. Her "seven clean days" then begin, after nightfall, on Sunday evening (i.e. the night between Sunday and Monday).*

Day of Week	Day of Month AV	Comment	
Tuesday	16	she becomes a **niddah** on Tuesday after nightfall or on Wednesday during daylight	
Wednesday	17		Day One
Thursday	18		Day Two
Friday	19		Day Three
Shabbat	20		Day Four
Sunday	21	before sunset: **hefsek taharah**	Day Five

A woman whose menstrual bleeding lasts longer than five days must wait to make her *hefsek taharah* until the day on which her bleeding ceases.

2. What is the right time of day for hefsek taharah?

The *hefsek taharah* must be performed before sunset (שקיעה), the times of which can be found in a reliable Jewish calendar. If her community prays *Ma'ariv* before sunset, she should perform the *bedikah* before *Ma'ariv*. On Friday afternoon or on the eve of Yom Tov, she should perform the *bedikah* before lighting the Shabbat or Yom Tov candles. However, if she was unable or forgot to make her *bedikah* beforehand, then she can still perform her *hefsek taharah* after lighting the candles and *Ma'ariv*, as long as it is before sunset (שקיעה).

3. The bedikah (בדיקה – examination)

A woman should wash her body, or at least around the genital area, with warm water. She is then ready to perform the *bedikah* as described in Chapter 3.2, p. 14.

After withdrawing the *bedikah*-cloth, she must carefully inspect it by daylight. If the cloth appears whitish or yellowish, without the smallest trace of a black or reddish speck, the *bedikah* is "clean." If there is any doubt about the color, a Rabbi should be consulted. (See Chapter 5.1, p. 28.)

If the *bedikah* was not perfectly "clean," she can repeat the checking until sunset (שקיעה). If she cannot achieve a "clean" *bedikah* before sunset, she must postpone the *hefsek taharah* to the following afternoon, with the consequent result that the "seven clean days" will also start a day later.

4. White underwear and bedding

After a successful *bedikah*, a woman must put on clean white underwear. Preferably, the sheets on her bed should also be white and clean until the end of the "seven clean days." (See Chapter 3.3, p. 15.)

5. Moch dachuk (מוך דחוק) – a final check for hefsek taharah

After a "clean" *bedikah* has been achieved, a woman should ascertain that there has been no further flow of blood between sunset and nightfall. She does this by inserting a fresh *bedikah*-cloth into her vagina, which should be left in place from sunset until nightfall. This second cloth is called a *moch dachuk* and is inspected in the same way as the first *bedikah*.

If the insertion of a *moch dachuk* causes irritation or any kind of difficulty, a Rabbi should be consulted.

6. *Hefsek taharah on Shabbat, Yom Tov, and Yom Kippur*

If the day of *hefsek taharah* turns out to be a Shabbat or Yom Kippur, a woman should wash herself either with cold water, or with water which has been heated on the previous day. On these days, as well as on Yom Tov, only the genital areas should be washed. Furthermore, this should done using her hand and not a wash cloth or sponge.

3
Counting the "Seven Clean Days"
(ספירת ז' נקיים)

From the evening after a successful hefsek taharah a woman can start counting her "seven clean days." The day on which the hefsek taharah was performed does not count as part of these "seven clean days." The "seven clean days" must be consecutive and free from any flow of blood from the uterus.

She does a bedikah twice a day, in order to verify that there is no blood in her vagina. She also wears white underwear and covers her bed with white bed linen during this period, to confirm that no bleeding has occurred between the bedikot.

Once all the bedikot have proved "clean," she may then go to the mikveh. She immerses herself after nightfall at the end of the seventh day (beginning of the eighth day).

1. *The bedikot (בדיקות – examinations) – when?*

During the "seven clean days," a woman must make a *bedikah* twice daily, once in the morning and once in the afternoon. The morning *bedikah* should preferably take place after sunrise (הנץ החמה), but not before daybreak (עלות השחר). The afternoon *bedikah* should be done before sunset (שקיעה).

It is important for a woman to make a *bedikah* twice daily.

However, if she was unable or forgot to make some of these *bedikot*, she can still continue to count her "seven clean days," provided she has completed her *hefsek taharah* (see Chapter 2.3) and has made at least one *bedikah* on the first day of her "seven clean days" and one on the last day.

If a woman finds it difficult to carry out any of the *bedikot* (due to dryness of the vagina or a wound), a Rabbi should be consulted.

It is useful to note the first of the "seven clean days" on a calendar.

Working Example continued (see Chapter 2.1)

Day of Week	Day of Month AV	Comment	
Tuesday	16	she becomes a *niddah* on Tuesday after nightfall or on Wednesday during daylight	
Wednesday	17		Day One
Thursday	18		Day Two
Friday	19		Day Three
Shabbat	20		Day Four
Sunday	21	before sunset: *hefsek taharah*	Day Five
Monday	22	1st day of the "seven clean days"	
Tuesday	23	2nd day of the "seven clean days"	
Wednesday	24	3rd day of the "seven clean days"	
Thursday	25	4th day of the "seven clean days"	
Friday	26	5th day of the "seven clean days"	
Shabbat	27	6th day of the "seven clean days"	
Sunday	28	7th day of the "seven clean days" on Sunday night after nightfall: *tevilah*	
Monday	29	(immersion in the *mikveh*)	

2. The bedikah (בדיקה) – how is it done?

The cloth used for the *bedikah* must be made from pure white cotton, wool, or linen, measuring approximately 7–8 cm square (3 inches square). A tampon may **not** be used. As the skin in the vagina is quite sensitive, the cloth must be soft, and it is therefore advisable to use pre-washed cloths.

Before the *bedikah*, both sides of the *bedikah*-cloth should be inspected to ensure that it is clean. The ideal position for making a *bedikah* is standing with one foot placed on a chair. She then inserts her finger, with the cloth wrapped around it, as deeply as possible into her vagina. Once inside, she rotates her finger in all directions and then slowly pulls it out, while still rotating it. It is important to check all crevices and folds of the vagina.

After completing the *bedikah*, the *bedikah*-cloth must be checked by daylight. The *bedikah* is considered to be "clean" if the cloth contains no red, reddish, or black dot and any discharge on the cloth has no reddish tinge to it. Any red, reddish, or black dot or reddish tinge will render the *bedikah* "unclean." Discharges which are wholly white, yellow, greenish, or bluish are "clean." However, if the discharge is brown or orange a Rabbi must be consulted. A Rabbi should also be consulted in the following situations:

- ☐ If she discovers a thread or dot of an "unclean" color which may not have originated from her body, or any congealed or dried matter of an "unclean" color.

- ☐ If there is a possibility that she has a wound in her womb or vagina.

It is also advisable not to use any pink or reddish toilet paper during this week, as tiny pieces of the paper could appear on the *bedikah*-cloth, and the woman may not find them easily distinguishable from actual drops of blood.

3. *White underwear and bedding*

During the "seven clean days" a woman must wear clean white underwear, and the bed linen should be clean and white. These should be checked daily for any possible "unclean" staining. (See Chapter 5.4, p. 29.)

4. *A failed bedikah*

If a *bedikah* is not "clean" or if bleeding occurs at any time during the "seven clean days," she must perform another *hefsek taharah* and begin counting the "seven clean days" again. This *hefsek taharah* may be performed on the same day without waiting the five days described in Chapter 2.1, as more than five days have already elapsed since she became a *niddah*. If the *hefsek taharah* is successful, she may start counting her "seven clean days" again from the following day.

4

Immersion in the Mikveh (Tevilah – טבילה)

*The modern mikveh is built with all the convenience and pri-
vate comfort expected in our times. It contains comfortable
rooms for bathing and other preparations.*

*The actual mikveh looks like a small indoor swimming pool
with steps leading into the heated water. The depth of the water
is approximately 120 cm (4 ft.), so that the person can stand in
it easily and immerse without difficulty.*

*A woman may immerse only in a mikveh which is regularly
checked by a rabbinic authority. A woman who uses any other
type of bath as a mikveh will remain a niddah.*

*The tevilah (immersion) is not performed in order to cleanse the
body physically. The laws of purity in the Torah are considered
chukkim (laws for which the human mind cannot find an apparent reason). Nevertheless, the observance of tevilah leads to
a feeling of spiritual renewal and holiness, the woman feeling
uplifted by the purifying waters.*

*When immersing, the mikveh water must simultaneously reach
all parts of her body, including all her hair. It is therefore necessary for the body to be thoroughly cleansed and for foreign substances and objects (חציצה), which are not part of her body, to be
removed.*

1. Immersion in the mikveh – when?

A woman immerses herself in the *mikveh* after nightfall, at the end of the "seven clean days" (the beginning of the eighth day). If she finds it very difficult to go to the *mikveh* after nightfall, e.g. the *mikveh* is very far or it is dangerous to go at night, she should consult a Rabbi.

If her husband is in town, a woman may not delay her immersion unless she has a compelling reason to do so. Even when the *tevilah* has to be postponed, still she may immerse herself only after nightfall.

A woman should try to ensure that even her closest friends and family do not know when she is going to the *mikveh* (out of צניעות, modesty).

2. Immersion in the mikveh – where?

A woman may immerse herself only in a *mikveh* which is under regular rabbinical supervision. Any other type of bath is invalid. If there is no possibility of immersing in such a *mikveh*, a Rabbi must be consulted as to which rivers, seas, or lakes may be used instead.

3. Preparing for the immersion (tevilah)

The water in the *mikveh* must be in contact with every part of the body during immersion. It is therefore crucial that the body is perfectly clean and free from any foreign substance or object. Detailed below are the precautions and preparations necessary to achieve a correct immersion in the *mikveh*.

Precautions on the day of *tevilah*

On the day of *tevilah* (i.e. the seventh day of the "seven clean days"), a woman should avoid handling sticky substances, e.g. dough. If she cannot avoid this, she must clean her hands and nails with great care as soon as she completes her task.

She should also avoid eating meat or anything else which leaves particles stuck between her teeth. However, on Shabbat, Yom Tov, Chol Hamoed, or Purim, meat may be eaten, but she must take extra care when cleaning her teeth.

Preparations before the *tevilah*

A. **Removing foreign objects** — A woman must remove all foreign objects, so that she is able to wash every part of herself and allow her whole body to be in direct contact with the water in the *mikveh* at the time of *tevilah*.

Examples of foreign objects are:

- ☐ Jewelry
- ☐ Contact lenses
- ☐ Hairpins
- ☐ Cotton wool in ears
- ☐ Dentures
- ☐ Bandaids, including the adhesive they leave on the skin
- ☐ Splinters, unless completely embedded in the skin

A Rabbi should be consulted with regard to temporary fillings of the teeth, plaster of Paris, artificial limbs, or any other foreign object which cannot, or must not, be removed.

B. **Cutting one's nails** — Both fingernails and toenails must be cut short. Then, any dirt under the nails, nail polish, and false nails, must be completely removed.

C. **Cleansing one's body before the *tevilah*** — After removing all foreign objects, a woman is ready to begin cleansing her body.

Every part of her body must be thoroughly washed, in a warm bath, with soap. Any dirt, coloring, make-up, and lipstick must be removed.

Her hair must be well shampooed and then rinsed thoroughly to remove all traces of shampoo. Afterwards, she must comb all the hair, including body hair, carefully, to ensure that there are no knots or tangles. This is to allow the water of the *mikveh* to cover every single hair.

A woman should use soap and shampoo which contains no moisturizer. Body lotion, conditioner, or any other additives which leave a residue or film on her body or hair must not be used.

A scab on a wound that has not healed completely is considered part of her body and does not have to be removed. However, a scab on a sore that has healed must be removed. Therefore, she should soak the scab in warm water, and if she can then remove it from the wound without causing any new bleeding, she must do so. Otherwise, the scab should be left alone.

Apart from the cleansing of the outer surfaces of the body, all creases, folds, and crevices of the body must also be thoroughly clean. Similarly, those parts of the body that are sometimes visible, e.g. teeth, must also be cleansed. Although these "concealed" parts of the body (בית הסתרים) need not actually come in contact with the water of the *mikveh*, they must still be clean like the rest of the body. A woman must therefore pay particular attention to her eyes, nose, indentations of the outer ear, navel, and any folds of skin.

She must brush her teeth well and, if necessary, also use a toothpick or a mouthwash. She should then rinse her mouth thoroughly so that nothing remains between her teeth. Thereafter, she may not eat until after her immersion, in order that her teeth remain clean.

Prior to her immersion she should use the toilet, and thereafter clean the private parts of her body once again.

All these preparations must be performed with the most precise attention to every detail. Anyone who finds it difficult to clean a certain part of the body must consult a Rabbi.

In order not to omit any of these preparations, it is advisable that they be carried out in a logical sequence. On page 26 we have printed a checklist. This can be used as it stands, or it can be adapted to suit each individual.

4. Preparing for the tevilah – when and where?

The preparations should be carried out before nightfall, as close as possible to *tevilah*. The *tevilah* itself may be performed only after nightfall. Therefore it is advisable to begin the preparations by day, and continue until nightfall.

Even if a woman can begin to prepare herself only after nightfall, she should not rush and should spend approximately one hour on her preparations. She should take care to relax and pay due attention to each detail. If possible, she should try at least to cut her nails before nightfall.

A woman can prepare herself either at home or at the *mikveh*. If she bathed at home, she should comb her hair and check her entire body again at the *mikveh*. Ideally, she should shower again briefly.

5. Tevilah on Friday night or at the beginning of Yom Tov

Should the time of *tevilah* coincide with Friday night, all preparations must be completed before the onset of Shabbat. However, she may immerse only after nightfall on Shabbat. Prior to her immersion, she must check her entire body and all her hair once again. After *tevilah*, she must take care not to wring her hair.

A woman should light the Shabbat candles before going to the *mikveh*. If it is necessary for her to perform a *melachah* (type of work that is prohibited on Shabbat) after lighting the candles, such as carrying her towel or driving, then she must expressly state, before lighting, that she does not want the Shabbat restrictions to apply to her with the lighting of the candles. (For details see page 58.) Obviously, she can defer the start of Shabbat only until the official onset of Shabbat. After this time, all work is forbidden. Alternatively, she could ask her husband to light the candles after she has left for the *mikveh*. Care should be taken not to light before the earliest time allowed. (See page 57.)

On Yom Tov she can light the candles after returning from the *mikveh* and before commencing the meal. The normal rules for lighting candles on Yom Tov must be followed, as detailed on page 57.

6. Tevilah on Motza'ei Shabbat or Yom Tov, or at the end of Tishah B'Av

Should the time of immersion coincide with the close of Shabbat or Yom Tov (followed by a weekday) or Tishah B'Av, the woman should complete all her preparations on the previous day (i.e. on *Erev Shabbat* or *Erev Yom Tov*, etc.). After nightfall, immediately prior to *tevilah*, she should briefly wash her body and hair again, comb all her hair, and brush her teeth. She must then check her body carefully. If she finds it difficult to make all the preparations on the previous day, she can do them immediately prior to her immersion after the end of Shabbat, Yom Tov, or Tishah B'Av. This, of course, should be done in the usual unhurried manner as described above in Section 4.

If the time of the *tevilah* falls on the second night of Yom Tov, all the preparations have to be made on the previous weekday, i.e. *Erev Yom Tov*. The same applies where *tevilah* takes place on *Motza'ei Yom Tov* which falls on Friday night or on Yom Tov which falls on *Motza'ei Shabbat*.

Example: *If Yom Tov falls on Monday and Tuesday and the tevilah is due to take place on Monday night after nightfall, the preparations should be made on Sunday before the onset of Yom Tov. Similarly, if Yom Tov falls on Sunday and the tevilah is due to take place on Motza'ei Shabbat, the preparations should be made on Erev Shabbat.*

Before *tevilah*, she must wash all the "concealed" parts of her body with warm water. (On Shabbat, she must use water which has been warmed before Shabbat.) The concealed parts of her body include those parts of the body which sweat profusely, or where dirt may collect, such as ears, eyes, nose, armpits, under the breasts, the navel, the private parts, between the toes, as well as other crevices and folds of the body. She should then check her whole body and all her hair, including body hair, very carefully.

The mouth and teeth must also be cleaned carefully. The woman may brush her teeth with a toothbrush but without toothpaste. If possible, the toothbrush should be set aside specially for Shabbat and Yom Tov. The toothbrush should not be wetted before or after brushing. Women whose gums always bleed when brushed should not use a toothbrush which causes bleeding. A toothpick may be used, but not if it causes bleeding.

Since one or more days will elapse between the preparations and *tevilah*, the woman must tie her hair back after her bath on *Erev Shabbat* or *Erev Yom Tov*, in a manner which will prevent it from knotting. A woman whose hair forms knots easily (e.g. curly hair) must consult a Rabbi.

A woman should also avoid working with sticky substances in the intervening day or days. If this is not possible, she must wash her hands with special care, immediately.

7. *Just before the tevilah*

Immediately prior to the immersion, the woman should check that all foreign objects (see page 18, 3A) have been removed. She must carefully inspect her body, both visually and by using her fingers, to check that no foreign substance is present. If anything is left on her body, her *tevilah* may be invalid and she will remain a *niddah*.

When going into the *mikveh*, special attention should be paid to the soles of the feet, where dirt or hairs adhere easily.

8. *The tevilah itself*

During immersion, a Jewish woman who is familiar with the laws of *tevilah*, usually the *mikveh* attendant, must be present. She must ensure that the entire body is under water at the same time. A woman remains a *niddah* if even just part of a single hair is not covered by the water.

As the water must make contact with the whole body, the following rules apply during *tevilah*:

- [ ] Feet should be apart.
- [ ] Arms should not be pressed against the body, and fists should not be clenched.
- [ ] Eyes may not be closed tightly, nor opened too wide.
- [ ] Mouth should be gently closed, but not too tightly. If possible, the top and bottom teeth should not be pressed together.
- [ ] Nose should not be held in any way.
- [ ] While submerging, she should bend forward slightly. Bending forward too much will cause parts of her body to become folded over.

Nobody may touch her while she is under water. If she needs somebody to hold her, a Rabbi should be consulted.

9. The blessing (berachah – ברכה)

The woman should immerse once in the manner described above. She should then fold her arms below her heart and say the following blessing while standing in the water:

בָּרוּךְ אַתָּה יְיָ אֱלֹהֵינוּ מֶלֶךְ הָעוֹלָם אֲשֶׁר קִדְּשָׁנוּ בְּמִצְוֹתָיו, וְצִוְּנוּ עַל הַטְּבִילָה

(Baruch Atah Adonay Elohaynu Melech ha-olam, asher kidshanu b'mitzvotav v'tzivanu al hatevilah – *Blessed are You, God, our Lord, King of the world, who has sanctified us with His commandments and commanded us concerning the immersion.*)

While saying the *berachah*, she must not look at her body. It is customary to dip once or twice more after reciting this blessing. If the woman has forgotten to say the blessing, she does not need to perform the *tevilah* again.

10. *After tevilah*

It is customary that, after the *tevilah*, the woman should be approached and touched by another Jewish woman before anyone else. Usually, the *mikveh* attendant will touch the woman after the immersion. Bathing or showering immediately after the *mikveh* should be avoided unless physical contact has already been made between husband and wife.

Checklist of preparations before immersion

1. Have you done your *bedikot* (internal examinations) today?

Before washing
2. Remove rings, earrings, and all other jewelry.
3. Remove any foreign objects such as contact lenses, hairpins, cotton wool, bandaids, etc.
4. Remove nail polish from fingernails and toenails.
5. Cut and clean fingernails and toenails.
6. Brush teeth.
7. Remove make-up and lipstick.
8. Clean ears, nose, and eyes.

When washing
9. Wash face well.
10. Wash body and hair thoroughly (paying special attention to the navel and other folds of skin on the body, as well as the holes of pierced ears, etc.).
11. Comb all hair on the head and body carefully.

If you cannot clean a part of your body properly (e.g. because of coloring, bandage, etc.) you must consult a Rabbi. Scabs must be soaked.

After washing
12. After relieving yourself, carefully wash private areas again.
13. Shower after the bath.

Just prior to immersion
14. If you have had your bath at home, shower briefly and comb your hair once again.
15. Check all over your body carefully once again. Ensure that all foreign objects (see 3 above) have been removed.

AFTER HAVING CAREFULLY COMPLETED ALL THE PREPARATIONS, YOU MAY THEN ENTER THE *MIKVEH*.

In the water

16. Immerse slightly bent forward and not standing erect. Do not bend over too far; this causes the skin to fold and crease.

17. When immersing:
    - ☐ Do not put your feet too close to one another.
    - ☐ Do not press your arms against your body. Do not clench your fists.
    - ☐ Do not close your eyes tightly. Do not open them too wide.
    - ☐ Do not close your mouth tightly, but close it gently.

18. Ensure that your entire body and every hair is submerged.

IF YOU HAVE FOLLOWED ALL THESE INSTRUCTIONS EXACTLY, YOU ARE NOT A *NIDDAH* ANYMORE. YOU ARE NOW READY TO RETURN TO YOUR HUSBAND.

5
Becoming a Niddah

1. When does a woman become a niddah?

Even the smallest amount of blood leaving the uterus will render the woman a *niddah*. It does not matter whether the bleeding occurs at the time when her period is due or at any other time, including during pregnancy.

The definition of blood which renders a woman a *niddah* is any red, reddish, or black discharge from the womb. If the color of the discharge is white, yellow, greenish, or bluish and contains no red, reddish, or black dot, she does not become a *niddah*. Any other color (e.g. brown) is questionable, and a Rabbi should be consulted. A Rabbi must also be consulted if blood is found in the urine.

2. Sensation of a discharge (זיבת דבר לח)

A woman who feels liquid flowing from her vagina should check her underwear and determine the color of the discharge (see 1 above). If she finds no discharge on her underwear, she should perform a *bedikah*.

A woman who frequently experiences vaginal discharge, and who has subsequently always found her *bedikot* "clean," does not need to check when feeling a discharge, unless she has a specific reason to believe that it is blood.

3. *Opening of the uterus* (פתיחת המקור)

A woman who experiences a sensation of her uterus opening has probably become a *niddah*. She must therefore make a *bedikah* immediately thereafter. If the discharge on the cloth is red, reddish, or black, she has become a *niddah*. In any other case, a Rabbi must be consulted, as it is possible that she may have become a *niddah*, although the *bedikah* is of a clean color. *Nowadays this opening sensation is very rarely felt.*

4. *Staining (ketem –* כתם*)*

When a woman discovers a blood stain on her body, under-clothes, or bedding, *without having experienced any sensation of vaginal discharge*, the following rules apply:

The woman does *not* become a *niddah* if the stain is:

- ☐ Smaller in area than the size of the circle printed on the next page, or
- ☐ Found on a completely colored background (e.g. on colored underwear), or
- ☐ Found in a place where it couldn't possibly have come from her vagina.

In all other cases, a Rabbi should be consulted. If a woman discovers blood on her toilet paper, a Rabbi should also be consulted.

What is relevant is not the shape of the stain but its total area. Several separate stains, each smaller than the size shown be-low, which a woman finds on her clothes or bed linen, will not render her a *niddah*. However, if they are found directly on her body, then it is the aggregate area of all the stains which must be considered. If the total area of all the stains equals or exceeds the area shown below, she has become a *niddah*.

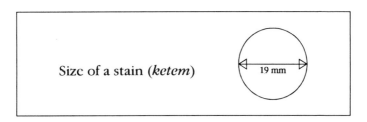

Size of a stain (*ketem*)   19 mm

It must be emphasised that on a *bedikah*-cloth, even the tiniest drop of blood will render the woman a *niddah*.

5. Gynecological examinations

After a gynecological examination of the uterus, a woman must inquire of the doctor whether he has opened her inner cervix – the place where the neck of the womb ends and the womb begins. If the inner cervix was opened, she must consult a Rabbi to ascertain whether she has become a *niddah*.

6. Birth or miscarriage

Every birth or miscarriage automatically renders the woman a *niddah* whether bleeding occurs or not. (See Chapter 9, page 49.)

6

Separation during the Time of Niddah

The Torah states: "Do not come close to a woman who is ritually unclean due to her menstruation" (Leviticus 18:19). This teaches us that during the time of niddah, not only are marital relations forbidden, but also other forms of contact.

These rules apply from the moment a woman becomes a niddah, until after tevilah in a mikveh. Similarly, at a time when there is doubt as to whether the woman has become a niddah, these rules must be kept until the matter is resolved, usually by rabbinical decision.

As explained in the introduction, it is impossible for the human intellect to comprehend the laws of the Torah. Yet it can be appreciated that the complete physical separation during the time of niddah will ensure that husband and wife learn to love one another in a manner which transcends physical love. They will form a bond based on a deep inner understanding and true love for each other.

1. *Physical contact and intimacy*

A husband and wife may not touch each other either directly or indirectly (i.e. with an object). Furthermore, they may not hand or directly throw anything to one another.

A husband and wife must not sit together on a movable item, unless a third person or a sizeable object is placed between

BREAD, FIRE, AND WATER

them and there is no risk of the spouses coming into contact with one another. An example of such a movable item would be a light bench, which is not fixed to the wall, where the movements of one spouse is felt by the other.

A ride solely for pleasure, such as a ride on a small boat, is allowed only if another person or a sizeable object is between them.

Intimate talk, or light-headed and flirtatious behavior, which may arouse desire, must be avoided.

The husband may not gaze at those parts of his wife's body which are usually covered.

2. In the bedroom

Husband and wife may neither sleep in the same bed nor in two separate beds which are touching. The gap between the beds should be wide enough to prevent the bedcovers from touching.

The husband may not sit or lie on his wife's bed even when she is not in the room. The wife, however, may sit on her husband's bed in his presence as long as he is not sitting on it at the same time. (See Section 1 above.) Lying on his bed is permitted only when her husband is not present.

They may not put clean bedding on each other's bed when the spouse is in the room. Putting on clean bedding when the other is not in the room is allowed, even if he or she is aware of it.

3. Mealtimes

When eating together, with nobody else present at the table, an object which would not otherwise be there, must be placed on the table between them. This will serve as a reminder not to become intimate.

Eating out of the same dish together, at the same time, is forbidden.

A husband may not eat his wife's leftover food on her plate, nor may he drink the leftovers in her glass in her presence. This only applies if he is aware that the food or drink are her leftovers. If the food or drink is moved to another container, or if she has left the room, he is permitted to finish her leftovers. She is permitted to eat or drink her husband's leftovers in all circumstances.

Pouring or serving drinks for one another should be done in a slightly different manner from the usual, e.g. by serving with the left hand (or right hand for a left-handed person) or by placing the cup a little further away. If the spouse is not present, then it may be done in the usual manner.

If possible, food should be served by the wife to her husband in a manner which is slightly different, as above.

A husband may not designate a cup or glass of wine for his wife, even if it is passed to her by a third person. The *Kiddush* cup may not be passed on to her by her husband, but she may take it herself and drink thereof.

4. During illness

Even when either the husband or wife is ill, all the laws of separation must be observed. If this is not possible, a Rabbi should be consulted.

7

The Expected Time of the Next Period (Vesset – וסת)

Most women have a fairly regular monthly cycle (except for pregnant and nursing women or those who are post-menopausal). As explained earlier, any blood which leaves the uterus causes a woman to become a niddah, even if it remains inside her body. Therefore the beginning of her period can easily go unnoticed. To avoid an inadvertent transgression of the laws of niddah, she or her husband must calculate the anticipated onset of her next period in advance.

For some women, this calculation will be exact, and for others, only approximate. For the purposes of these rules, a distinction is made between a regular cycle and an irregular cycle, and is discussed in detail in this chapter.

1. Introduction

It is important for a woman to know when the onset of her last period occurred, so that she can calculate when her next period is due. She should, therefore, note down the Hebrew date and whether the period started during the day or at night.

"Night" in this context begins at sunset (שקיעה) and ends at sunrise (הנץ החמה), while "day" lasts from sunrise to sunset.

BREAD, FIRE, AND WATER

2. Separation and bedikah on the expected date of the next period

During the "night" or the "day" when the next period is expected, marital relations are forbidden.* Couples also avoid embracing and kissing.

At least one *bedikah* must be made during that "day" or "night," in order to ascertain whether the period has started or not. A woman may find it useful to wear white underwear during that time. Once this time has passed without the onset of menstruation and providing that the *bedikah* was "clean," marital relations are permitted again.

3. Introduction to regular and irregular cycles

The calculation of the expected time differs considerably, depending on whether one is dealing with a regular (וסת קבוע) or irregular (וסת שאינו קבוע) cycle. Nowadays, most women have what is defined in these rules as an irregular cycle, and this, therefore, will be dealt with first.

Although the majority of women will have an irregular cycle, every couple must acquaint themselves with the rules for determining of a regular cycle in Section 5. After each period, a woman must ascertain whether she is still considered to have an irregular cycle or if she has assumed a regular cycle.

4. The irregular cycle (וסת שאינו קבוע)

In the case of an irregular cycle, separation and *bedikah* (see

---

* Many also keep these laws for an extra "day" or "night" before the anticipated time of the next period. This would mean that when the expected time for the period is during the "day," the "night" before is added, and if it is expected during the "night," the "day" before is added (עונת אור זרוע).

Section 2 above), are required on the following three dates, as each of these is regarded to be a likely date for the start of the next period:

A. After the same interval (הפלגה)

A woman must calculate the interval between the commencements of her two previous periods. She counts from the first day of the period before last to the first day of her last period. She then counts that same number of days from the first day of her last period.

If her last period started at night, the laws of separation and *bedikah* must be observed during the night of the calculated date. If her last period started during the day, then the separation and *bedikah* must be observed during the day of the calculated date. As in Section 1 above, "night" begins at sunset and ends at sunrise, and "day" lasts from sunrise until sunset.

Example: *The period before last commenced at some time on 20 Tammuz, and the last period commenced on the night of 17 Av. Including the days of the start of both periods, there are 27 days between the two periods. The expected date will therefore be 27 days later, which will be 13 Elul. Thus, separation and bedikah must be observed during the night of that date. Please refer to the calendar printed on page 40.*

B. On Day 30 (עונה בינונית)

The next period is also expected on the 30th day from the start of the last period (that day included). In contrast with the night or day separation of the previous and following sections, the "Day 30" separation should be observed for the full 24-hour period of that day, from sunset to sunset.*

Example: *The last period started at some time on the 17th of Av. Day 30 is on 16 Elul. In the calendar printed below, 16 Elul is a Thursday and, therefore, separation and bedikah must be observed from sunset on Wednesday evening until sunset on Thursday evening.*

At the end of the 24 hours, the wife must confirm to her husband that her period has not yet commenced before resuming intimacy.

C. On the same day of the month (יום החודש)

The next period is also expected on the same day of the Hebrew month as the last period. As in Section A above, separation and *bedikah* are observed during the night or day, depending on when the last period started.

It is useful to appreciate that Hebrew months have either 29 or 30 days. If the current month has 29 days, the "same day of the month" will coincide with "Day 30" (see Section B). If it has 30 days, the "same day of the month" will be the day after "Day 30."

Example: *The last period commenced during the night of 17 Av. The same day of the following month would be 17 Elul, a Friday according to the calendar shown below. From Thursday evening (sunset – שקיעה), until Friday morning (sunrise – הנץ החמה) the above laws of separation and bedikah must be observed. If the period had started during the day, the couple must separate from sunrise on Friday morning until sunset on Friday night.*

---

* Some keep Day 30 and Day 31.

TAMMUZ				
Sun	1	8	15	22	29
Mon	2	9	16	23
Tue	3	10	17	24
Wed	4	11	18	25
Thu	5	12	19	26
Fri	6	13	**20**	27
Sat	7	14	21	28

A V					
Sun		7	14	21	28
Mon	1	8	15	22	29
Tue	2	9	16	23	30
Wed	3	10	**17**	24
Thu	4	11	18	25
Fri	5	12	19	26
Sat	6	13	20	27

ELUL					
Sun		5	12	19	26
Mon		6	**13**	20	27
Tue		7	14	21	28
Wed	1	8	15	22	29
Thu	2	9	**16**	23
Fri	3	10	**17**	24
Sat	4	11	18	25

Very often, a woman with an irregular cycle will know that she is unlikely to bleed before a certain number of days have elapsed. After this time, she has her "unsafe" time, during which her period is likely to occur. It is recommended that, in addition to the *bedikah* and separation on the days calculated, as above, a woman should also check on these "unsafe" days, shortly before having marital relations, to ensure that her period has not yet started.

Summary of working example: *A woman with an irregular cycle knows that the earliest time her period could start is 26 days after the onset of her last period. The period before last began on 20 Tammuz, and the last one during the night of 17 Av (an interval of 27 days).*

She is therefore required to observe the laws of separation and bedikah on the night of 13 Elul (see 4A above), as well as on 16 Elul (as in 4B), and also on the night of 17 Elul (as in 4C). Obviously, if her new period starts before any of these dates, they become irrelevant.

It is commendable for the woman to check from 12 Elul onwards (26 days after last period), shortly before having marital relations, to confirm that her period has not yet begun.

5. *The regular cycle* (וסת קבוע)

A cycle is considered regular if:

☐ Three consecutive periods occur with a repeating pattern (as defined later), and

☐ All three occasions occur during the same half of the day (i.e. day or night).

A repeating pattern occurs in either of the following two cases:

☐ *The same day of the Jewish month* (יום החודש): Three consecutive periods commence on the same date of a Jewish month (e.g. 10 Nissan, 10 Iyar, 10 Sivan), or

☐ *The same interval* (וסת הפלגה): During three consecutive cycles, the number of days between the start of the period and the start of the previous period is equal. Obviously three cycles of equal length can only be ascertained after four periods.

Once a regular cycle has been established, the time of her expected period is easily determined. She need, therefore, observe the laws of separation and *bedikah*, as described above, only on the expected day or night, as appropriate. In order for intimacy to be resumed after the period of separation, she must confirm to her husband that her period has not yet started.

In addition to the regular cycles mentioned above, any regular pattern which occurs three consecutive times may be considered as a regular cycle. These situations are rare, but below are a few brief examples of these patterns.

- ☐ 10 Nissan, 11 Iyar, 12 Sivan [one month plus a day] (וסת החודש בדילוג)

- ☐ 10 Nissan, 10 Sivan, 10 Av [every second month] (וסת החודש בסירוג)

- ☐ Intervals of 25, 26, and 27 days [interval plus a day] (וסת הפלגה בדילוג)

- ☐ Three times on the same day, e.g. every third Sunday for three consecutive times (after the fourth time, this will be a regular cycle with the same interval) (וסת ימי שבוע שווים)

- ☐ Three times after the same physical symptom (וסת הגוף), as explained below in Section 7

If there is any doubt as to the occurrence, a Rabbi should be consulted.

6. Breaking a regular cycle

In order for an established regular cycle to be broken, three consecutive periods must occur without any flow of blood at the expected time of the regular cycle.

After the first and second occasions when the regular cycle is broken, she must still observe the dates of separation and *bedikah* of that regular cycle, as well as the dates for the new irregular cycle.*

Once the regular cycle has been broken three times, she can ignore it, and only the dates for the irregular cycle apply. As long as no new regular cycle is established, the previous broken regular cycle will be re-established as soon as it recurs even once.

7. *Premenstrual physical symptoms* (וסת הגוף)

Some women experience specific physical symptoms before the onset of menstruation. These could include very frequent sneezing, yawning, or burping, certain pains in the abdomen or an unusual sensation of heaviness in the limbs or the head. If a woman notices that her period starts shortly after any of these symptoms occur, she must then expect her following period after any subsequent occurrence of the same symptom. She must then keep the laws relating to *bedikah* and separation at this time. If this pattern repeats itself three consecutive times, she has established a regular cycle.

If, as well as having premenstrual physical symptoms, she also has a regular pattern as in Section 5 above, then she is considered to have a regular cycle which is established by a combination of repeating pattern and same physical symptom (וסת המורכב). In this case, she need only apply the laws of separation and *bedikah* if that symptom coincides with that same interval or day of the month.

---

* Except for Day 30 (see Section 4B) which need not be observed, as long as she is still observing the separations for the regular cycle.

A woman who experiences such premenstrual physical symptoms should consult a Rabbi for details.

8. During pregnancy and breastfeeding

During the first three months of pregnancy, a woman with a regular cycle must still observe the rules relating to a regular cycle. From the fourth month and until after she has ceased breastfeeding, a woman need not observe her regular cycle. This means that if she starts to menstruate during this time, she must calculate her period in accordance with the laws pertaining to an irregular cycle. (See Section 4 above.)

When she has ceased breastfeeding, she must once again calculate her regular cycle as she did before her pregnancy. So if, for example, menstruation used to occur after a fixed interval, she must anticipate her next period at that same interval, and if it used to occur on the same day of the month, she must anticipate her next period on that day of the month.

9. Recording of the cycles

In order to calculate the onset of the next period, and to be able to recognize whether she has established a regular cycle, the Hebrew date of the onset of her period should be noted. A record should also be kept of whether it commenced during the day or at night. It is also advisable that the calculated dates for the onset of next month's period be written down immediately.

8
The Bride

1. Before the wedding – general rules

Every bride (irrespective of age or whether she has been married previously) must make *hefsek taharah*, count the "seven clean days," and go to the *mikveh* prior to her wedding. A bride may perform *hefsek taharah* on the day her menstruation ceases and does not need to wait five days from the beginning of her period. Unlike all other *tevilot* which must be done after nightfall, a bride may go to the *mikveh* during the day, but, obviously, no earlier than the eighth day.

A bride may perform *hefsek taharah* only once the date of her wedding has been set. A virgin carrying out her *bedikot* should insert the *bedikah*-cloth only as far as the hymen, so as not to tear it.

The bride's immersion should preferably not take place more than four days prior to her wedding. She should therefore time her *hefsek taharah* accordingly.

2. Before the wedding – problem situations

A Rabbi must be consulted in any of the following situations:

□ When the seventh day of the "seven clean days" will fall on the day of her wedding.

□ When the wedding is postponed since, in certain circumstances, the "seven clean days" may have to be counted again.

□ If the bride is unable to go to the *mikveh* before her wedding, or if she becomes a *niddah* before marital relations have taken place for the first time. In both cases the couple must observe all the laws of *niddah*. Additionally, they are forbidden to remain alone in a closed room, even during the day, until the bride has immersed in the *mikveh* (יחוד).

3. After the wedding – general rules

If the bride is a virgin, husband and wife must separate immediately after the first intercourse has taken place, even if there is no hymeneal bleeding. All the laws of *niddah* apply with the following exception. She may perform *hefsek taharah* on the fourth day, provided that her period has not yet begun. The fifth day can then count as the first of her "seven clean days," in contrast with a usual *niddah* who must wait until the fifth day.

If the woman experiences pain during the second intercourse, she should check the sheet for any traces of blood. If she finds a stain of an "unclean" color, she must apply the laws as after the first marital relations. Again, she may perform *hefsek taharah* on the fourth day and count her "seven clean days" from the fifth day, providing her period has not yet begun. These rules apply as long as she experiences pain during intercourse.

If she feels pain but finds no blood, she remains *tehorah*

(טהורה – pure) and does not have to separate from her husband.

4. After the wedding – special rules

As soon as intercourse is pain-free, a woman with an irregular cycle (see Chapter 7.4, page 37) should take steps to confirm that intercourse does not induce menstruation. She does this by making a *bedikah* on her "unsafe days" (see p. 40) before and after intercourse on three consecutive occasions. The husband should also wipe himself with a white cloth and check it for any traces of blood.

If either spouse finds any trace of blood, the woman becomes a *niddah*, and they must consult a Rabbi *before* resuming marital relations.

9
Childbirth

A woman in labor becomes a *niddah* if she has a show of blood or when she can no longer walk unaided. If the contractions stop – i.e. it is a false labor – a woman is not a *niddah* provided that no bleeding has occurred.

After birth, or a miscarriage, a woman can perform *hefsek taharah* and count the "seven clean days" once she has stopped bleeding. Usually, this does not happen until some time later. The earliest she is permitted to make *hefsek taharah* is on the fifth day after the birth of a boy, and on the seventh day after the birth of a girl. In the case of a miscarriage, where the sex of the child is not known, the rules follow that for a girl, and *hefsek taharah* can be made from the seventh day onwards. (See Leviticus, Chapter 12.)

There are various laws concerning giving birth on Shabbat or Yom Tov. The parents-to-be should consult a Rabbi regarding these laws, preferably at the beginning of the ninth month of pregnancy.

10

Consulting the Rabbi

W hen feeling unwell or when a routine check-up is required, one visits the doctor. Although the person may have basic knowledge about the health of the human body, he or she will still seek the advice of a specialist. Hence, although one may feel uncomfortable on the first occasion that one sees a gynecologist, nevertheless one goes, as it is vital for one's health. After the second or third visit, one becomes accustomed to it, feels more at ease, and such visits become part of everyday life.

Our spiritual health is as important as our physical health. Most of us do not master the laws of *niddah* in their entirety. Therefore, we need to consult a specialist – the Rabbi. At first, it may be embarrassing to consult a Rabbi and to present him with a *bedikah*-cloth, or even an item of underwear, for inspection. It feels like an invasion of one's privacy. But can we really afford to ignore our spiritual well-being? Will we be able to justify our actions before God? But, just like the first visit to the gynecologist, the first consultation with one's Rabbi must go ahead. Initial inhibitions are overcome, and consulting a Rabbi ceases to be a source of embarrassment.

Needless to say, the Rabbi, like a doctor, will treat all such consultations with total confidentiality.

When a doubt arises as to any law of *niddah*, it is wrong to take the law into one's own hand and to decide a matter stringently simply to avoid consulting a Rabbi. This is certainly not God's wish. Unfortunately, there are many women who eventually come to realize that for many years they were either too lenient or too strict about some of these laws, simply because they did not dare to consult a Rabbi.

The advice of an experienced Rabbi is not only limited to the minutiae of these laws. Often women have been helped by a Rabbi's advice in diverse ways, e.g. how to conceive or to be made aware at an early stage of diseases such as tumors and internal bleeding.

11
The Jewish Family

At the time of the First Temple, approximately 2500 years ago, King Chizkiyahu ruled over the Jewish people. About him is written, "And he did what was correct in the eyes of God, just like his father David had done... In God the Lord of Israel he trusted, and after him there was none like him in all the Kings of Judea, and those before him as well" (II Kings, Chapter 18).

And yet Chapter 20 describes how King Chizkiyahu becomes seriously ill. The prophet Yeshayahu tells him that he will die. The Talmud relates that the prophet also informed him that he would have no portion in the World to Come. Chizkiyahu is shocked, as all his life he has striven to follow the word of God and he cannot understand why he deserves such harsh punishment.

The Talmud explains that the prophet tells him, "Because by staying a bachelor you have not procreated children." The king replies: "I did not marry, because I knew that one of my descendants would cause the entire Jewish nation to commit idolatry." Thereupon, Yeshayahu responds, "It is your duty to fulfill the word of God and not to interfere with his ways.

God's commandment to us, to be fruitful and multiply, is a law you must obey despite your altruistic reasoning" (*Talmud Berachot* 10a).

This is a very powerful illustration of the will of God, as regards one's obligation to raise a family. Decisions to cease or delay having children must not be taken lightly. Should this present any problem, one must consult a Rabbi to clarify whether contraceptives may be used and which methods are permitted. The Rabbi will be most understanding and supportive. Under no circumstances, may one rely solely on the recommendation of the doctor or on the advice of a friend who herself was advised by a Rabbi.

By entrusting us with the procreation of mankind and by allowing us to participate in Creation, God is placing a miracle into our hands. By bringing a life into this world and directing our energies towards that life, we forge a path, from generation to generation, forever. Only through our children can we attempt to shape the future of the Jewish nation.

Sometimes in old age, we may start to regret the lack of purpose in our lives but, by then, it is too late. Then we long for the love and affection of children to ease the loneliness of old age, and yearn for the support and protection of the next generation.

We are like the flame of a candle. Lighting other candles will not diminish any of our own light. We must pass on our "light" to our children, so that they, in turn, can continue to illuminate the world after our passing.

Accordingly, let each one of us contribute to the expansion of our people and to the swelling of the ranks of the Jewish nation. Our health, and that of our children, rests in God's hands. "**See now, that I, I am the one and no other lord is** with me, I remove life and I give life, I smote and I will heal, and from my hand there is no savior" (*Deuteronomy* 32:39).

Let the blessing of God strengthen you in your holy and rewarding roles as parents of Jewish children.

The Laws of Lighting Candles for Shabbat and Yom Tov

12

Lighting Candles for Shabbat and Yom Tov

God said to Moshe, "I have a beautiful gift in my treasury: the Shabbat, which I would like to give to the Jewish people. Tell them about it" (Talmud Shabbat 10b). We are indeed fortunate to have been given the Shabbat, which elevates us and allows us to rise above our daily routine.

As Shabbat enters, we can feel the light of the candles fill the air with holiness. The Kiddush, the Shabbat meal, and the Shabbat songs uplift us further.

Rabbi Yossi, the son of Rabbi Yehudah says "Two angels accompany a man on his way home from the synagogue on a Friday night. One of them is good and the other is bad. When he enters his house and finds the candles burning, the table set, and the room tidy, the good angel says 'May it be His will that the next Shabbat should be the same!' And against his will, the bad angel responds Amen" (Talmud Shabbat 119b).

It is not surprising, therefore, that many Jewish families light the Shabbat candles, although they do not keep all the other laws of Shabbat. These homes will experience at least a little of the special atmosphere of Shabbat.

May it be His will that we will soon merit the fulfillment of the promise mentioned in the Talmud (Shabbat 118). Rabbi Shimon, the son of Yochai says "If the Jewish people twice keep the Shabbat properly, they shall merit immediate redemption."

BREAD, FIRE, AND WATER

1. Who lights?

Every Jewish person is obligated to kindle lights in honor of Shabbat and Yom Tov. The lights may be oil lamps, but most people find it more convenient to use candles.

This obligation falls primarily on the housewife, who lights on behalf of the whole household. If she is unable to light, then her husband or another person must do so, instead of her.

2. How many candles does one light?

It is customary to light at least two candles. Many women have the custom to light one extra candle for each child.

3. When does one light the candles?

For Shabbat: The time for lighting the candles starts from *Pelag Haminchah* (פלג המנחה) and ends a few minutes before sunset (שקיעה). After this time it is forbidden to light the candles. The times of *Pelag Haminchah* and sunset vary according to the length of the day and geographical location. These times can be found in some Jewish calendars, or any Rabbi will gladly help.

In communities where *Ma'ariv* is said before sunset, Shabbat starts with the Friday night prayers, at the end of *Lechah Dodi*, and the candles must be lit before then.

For Yom Tov: On Yom Tov the candles may be lit even after Yom Tov has come in, provided that one has an existing flame from which to light.

On the second night of Yom Tov, the candles should be lit after nightfall, as one is not allowed to prepare from the first day of Yom Tov for the second. If either day of Yom Tov coincides with Shabbat, then the rules for Shabbat will apply, and the candles must be lit before Shabbat comes in.

4. Doing creative work or eating after kindling

Once a woman has lit her candles for Shabbat or Yom Tov, she must observe all the restrictions of that day, even if it is still some time until sunset.

If she knows that she still has something important to do, which would involve her performing a *melachah*, she should expressly state before lighting that she wants the Shabbat or Yom Tov restrictions to apply to her only at the latest times for the commencement of Shabbat or Yom Tov, as detailed in Section 3 above.

Similarly, once she has lit the candles, she may not eat until *Kiddush*, unless she expressly states before lighting that Shabbat or Yom Tov should not yet start for her, as above.

Unlike a woman, a man does not automatically start his Shabbat or Yom Tov with the lighting of the candles. He therefore may perform a *melachah* or eat until the time of the *Ma'ariv* prayer or until the official start of Shabbat or Yom Tov (see *luach*), if earlier.

If candles are lit well before sunset (but, of course after the earliest time as in 3 above), one should try to ensure that at least one member of the household accepts upon himself the restrictions of Shabbat with the lighting. Otherwise, it would not be apparent that the candles are being lit specifically for Shabbat.

5. Which blessing (berachah) is recited?

When lighting the Shabbat candles one says:

בָּרוּךְ אַתָּה יְיָ אֱלֹהֵינוּ מֶלֶךְ הָעוֹלָם אֲשֶׁר קִדְּשָׁנוּ בְּמִצְוֹתָיו, וְצִוָּנוּ לְהַדְלִיק נֵר שֶׁל שַׁבָּת

(Baruch Atah Adonay Elohaynu Melech ha-olam, asher kidshanu b'mitzvotav v'tzivanu l'hadlik ner shel Shabbat – *Blessed are You, God, our Lord, King of the world, who has sanctified us with His commandments and commanded us to kindle a light of Shabbat.*)

When lighting the Yom Tov candles one says:

בָּרוּךְ אַתָּה יְיָ אֱלֹהֵינוּ מֶלֶךְ הָעוֹלָם אֲשֶׁר קִדְּשָׁנוּ בְּמִצְוֹתָיו, וְצִוָּנוּ לְהַדְלִיק נֵר שֶׁל יוֹם טוֹב

(Baruch Atah Adonay Elohaynu Melech ha-olam, asher kidshanu b'mitzvotav v'tzivanu l'hadlik ner shel Yom Tov – *Blessed are You, God, our Lord, King of the world, who has sanctified us with His commandments and commanded us to kindle a light of Yom Tov.*)

When Yom Tov falls on Shabbat one says:

בָּרוּךְ אַתָּה יְיָ אֱלֹהֵינוּ מֶלֶךְ הָעוֹלָם אֲשֶׁר קִדְּשָׁנוּ בְּמִצְוֹתָיו, וְצִוָּנוּ לְהַדְלִיק נֵר שֶׁל שַׁבָּת וְשֶׁל יוֹם טוֹב

(Baruch Atah Adonay Elohaynu Melech ha-olam, asher kidshanu b'mitzvotav v'tzivanu l'hadlik ner shel Shabbat v'shel Yom Tov – *Blessed are You, God, our Lord, King of the world, who has sanctified us with His commandments and commanded us to kindle a light of Shabbat and of Yom Tov.*)

When lighting the Yom Kippur candles one says:

בָּרוּךְ אַתָּה יְיָ אֱלֹהֵינוּ מֶלֶךְ הָעוֹלָם אֲשֶׁר קִדְּשָׁנוּ בְּמִצְוֹתָיו, וְצִוָּנוּ לְהַדְלִיק נֵר שֶׁל יוֹם הַכִּפּוּרִים

(Baruch Atah Adonay Elohaynu Melech ha-olam, asher kidshanu b'mitzvotav v'tzivanu l'hadlik ner shel Yom haKipurim – *Blessed are You, God, our Lord, King of the world, who has sanctified us with His commandments and commanded us to kindle a light of Yom Kippur.*)

When Yom Kippur falls on Shabbat one says:

בָּרוּךְ אַתָּה יְיָ אֱלֹהֵינוּ מֶלֶךְ הָעוֹלָם אֲשֶׁר קִדְּשָׁנוּ בְּמִצְוֹתָיו, וְצִוָּנוּ לְהַדְלִיק נֵר שֶׁל שַׁבָּת וְשֶׁל יוֹם הַכִּפּוּרִים

(Baruch Atah Adonay Elohaynu Melech ha-olam, asher kidshanu b'mitzvotav v'tzivanu l'hadlik ner shel Shabbat v'shel Yom haKipurim – *Blessed are You, God, our Lord, King of the world, who has sanctified us with His commandments and commanded us to kindle a light of Shabbat and of Yom Kippur.*)

For Yom Tov, except for the last two days of Passover, many women add the following *berachah*:

בָּרוּךְ אַתָּה יְיָ אֱלֹהֵינוּ מֶלֶךְ הָעוֹלָם שֶׁהֶחֱיָנוּ וְקִיְּמָנוּ וְהִגִּיעָנוּ לַזְּמַן הַזֶּה

(Baruch Atah Adonay Elohaynu Melech ha-olam, shehecheyanu v'kiymanu v'higi-anu lazman hazeh – *Blessed are You, God, our Lord, King of the world, who has kept us alive and sustained us and enabled us to reach this time.*)

6. When is the blessing said?

She should say the blessing after she has lit all the candles and put the match down. She should cover her eyes while reciting the blessing, so as not to see the lit candles.

On Yom Tov, some women have the custom to recite the blessing immediately before lighting the candles. In such cases, they should be careful to place the match down gently so as not to extinguish it directly, as extinguishing fire is forbidden on Yom Tov.

After lighting, it is customary for women to say a prayer for peace in their house and for children who will follow the ways of the Torah.

7. Where to light when not dining at home

If one is eating out Friday night but still sleeping at home, the candles should be lit at home. (See Sections 3 and 4 above regarding the earliest time for lighting and doing a *melachah* afterwards.) In such circumstances,

- ☐ **Either** the candles should be long enough to burn until one returns, when one should sit down by them and enjoy their light, e.g. by eating something

- ☐ **Or** one should sit and enjoy the candles for a short while after it starts to get dark. This can be done either before leaving the home or on the way back from the synagogue, as long as it has started to get dark.

If the candles might extinguish before one's return, and none of the above is possible, then the obligation to light can also be fulfilled by switching on the electric lights in the house for Shabbat. Again, the lights should not go off with the Shabbat-clock before one comes back.

Although some have the custom to light where they will be eating, it is preferable to light at home as above.

8. Lighting the candles in the hospital

When a married woman is not at home for Shabbat or Yom Tov, her husband should light. Although technically, a married woman who is in the hospital need not light, if there is some light in her room, because her husband is lighting at home, it is still customary for her to light in her room, if possible. If the hospital does not allow open flames, two flashlights or other electric lights may be used. The lighting must be in her room, and there is no point in lighting in an adjacent room, e.g. the nurses' office, if no light will shine into her room.

The Laws of Separating
Challah from Dough

13

The Separation of Challah from Dough

"You must separate the first portion of your kneading as a dough offering. It is very much like the elevated gift that is taken from the granary. From the beginning of the kneading, you must give an elevated gift to God, throughout your generations" (Numbers 15:20-21).

The Sefer HaChinunch, in mitzvah 385, provides the following insight into this commandment. "As man survives on food, of which bread is the most basic, God, by giving us a mitzvah which is connected to the making of bread, has provided us with a regularly recurring mitzvah. By taking challah, as this mitzvah is often referred to, a special blessing will rest on our bread and will also give us spiritual reward. Thus, our bread will become food for both our body and soul."

Introduction

The mitzvah of taking *challah* involves separating a small piece of dough from any dough belonging to a Jew, which is made of wheat, barley, spelt, oats, or rye. The separated piece of dough is called *challah*. In days of yore, when the laws of purity were kept properly, this *challah* was given to the *Cohen*. Nowadays, the *challah* must be burned, as even a *Cohen* may not eat it.

It is forbidden to eat any of the dough or baked product from which *challah* has not been taken. This applies to all dough irrespective of whether it will be used for bread, biscuits, or cake.

1. Who takes challah?

The mitzvah of taking *challah* applies to every Jew, but women have the primary obligation to perform this mitzvah. If, however, the woman is unable to take *challah* herself, then she may ask someone else (not a child) to take *challah* on her behalf.

2. From which dough?

a) There is no requirement at all to take *challah* in either of the following cases:

- ☐ Where there is less then 1.2 kg (2 lbs. 10 oz.) of flour in the dough, *or*

- ☐ Where no part of the dough will be baked in an oven or cooked in a pan without any other liquid, e.g. dough to be used for deep-fried doughnuts or *kreplach*.

b) In the following circumstances, *challah* must be taken but without a *berachah*:

- ☐ Where the flour in the dough is more than 1.2 kg but less then 2.25 kg* (5 lbs.), *or*

- ☐ The dough contains no water, olive oil, honey, milk, or wine.

---

* Some have the custom to recite a *berachah* from 1⅔ kg (3 lbs. 11 oz.) and more.

c) *Challah* must be taken with a *berachah*, if **all** the following conditions are met:

- ☐ The dough is made from 2.25 kg[*] (5 lbs.) of flour or more

- ☐ The dough contains any of the following: water, olive oil, honey, milk, wine

- ☐ At least a small part of the dough is to be baked in an oven or in a pan, without any other liquid.

3. When is challah taken?

If the dough is thick, as it would normally be for bread, *challah* is separated before baking. If the dough is of a liquid consistency, e.g. cake dough, it is separated after baking. If a woman forgot to take *challah* from a thick dough before it was baked, she must do so afterwards.

On Shabbat one is not permitted to separate *challah*. If she forgot to separate *challah* before Shabbat, then a piece of the baked product should be retained until Shabbat has ended, when *challah* should then be taken from this piece. The rest can then be eaten on Shabbat. This is permitted for a dough kneaded outside Eretz Yisrael (חוץ לארץ). In Eretz Yisrael, however, this may not be done, and one may not eat any of it until after Shabbat when *challah* is taken.

The same applies on Yom Tov for a dough which was kneaded before Yom Tov. If a dough is kneaded on Yom Tov, *challah* is taken on that day (even in Eretz Yisrael) and burnt after Yom Tov.

---

[*] Some have the custom to recite a *berachah* from 1⅔ kg (3 lbs. 11 oz.) and more.

BREAD, FIRE, AND WATER

4. How is it taken?

A piece of dough, roughly the size of half an egg, is separated as *challah* from the dough.

Where relevant (see 2 above), the following *berachah* is recited when separating *challah*.

בָּרוּךְ אַתָּה יְיָ אֱלֹהֵינוּ מֶלֶךְ הָעוֹלָם אֲשֶׁר קִדְּשָׁנוּ בְּמִצְוֹתָיו, וְצִוָּנוּ לְהַפְרִישׁ חַלָּה מִן הָעִסָּה

(Baruch Atah Adonay Elohaynu Melech ha-olam, asher kidshanu b'mitzvotav v'tzivanu l'hafrish challah min ha'isah – *Blessed are You, God, our Lord, King of the world, who has sanctified us with His commandments and commanded us to separate challah from the dough.*)

Afterwards one says, "This is *challah*." The piece of *challah* is then burned or, if more convenient, wrapped well and placed in the garbage can. If the separated *challah* falls back into the dough and gets mixed up with it, a Rabbi must be consulted.

5. Combination of several doughs (צירוף)

If a number of similar types of dough are made, which individually do not have the required amount of flour but put together they do, then they have to be joined together in order for *challah* to be taken. This is done by placing all the doughs or cakes in one container or by placing them on a cloth and covering them all with the same cloth. *Challah* is then taken as appropriate.

In cases of non-similar types of dough which individually do not add up to the required amount, a Rabbi must be consulted.

Glossary of Hebrew Terms

Bedikah	internal examination of the vagina, to check for the presence of blood
Berachah	blessing
Challah	piece of dough to be separated from any dough made of wheat, barley, spelt, oats, or rye
Chol Hamoed	the intermediate days of the Festivals of Passover and Sukkot
Chukkim	Torah statutes
Hefsek taharah	internal examination of the vagina and laws pertaining to it, to establish that menstruation has ceased
Ketem	stain
Kiddush	blessing on wine, recited at the beginning of Shabbat and Yom Tov meals
Kosher	accepted by Jewish law as fit for consumption or use
Luach	Jewish calendar
Ma'ariv	evening prayers
Melachah	creative work that is prohibited on Shabbat or on Jewish festivals
Mikveh	ritual bath
Mitzvah	commandment of God
Moch dachuk	cloth inserted into the vagina on the day of *hefsek taharah* to establish that there is no flow of blood between sunset and nightfall

Motza'ei Shabbat	the night following Shabbat, i.e. Saturday night
Motza'ei Yom Tov	the night following a Jewish festival
Niddah	ritual state of impurity from the moment blood flows from a woman's uterus until after she immerses in the ritual bath
Shabbat	Saturday
Tehorah	ritually pure, "clean," i.e. not *niddah*
Tevilah	immersion in the ritual bath
Tishah B'Av	the Ninth of Av, a fast day commemorating the destruction of the Holy Temple
Yom Kippur	the Day of Atonement
Yom Tov	Jewish festival day

Index

Hebrew Notes

Hebrew Notes
חזקת הבית

THE LAWS OF NIDDAH
Chapter 2: THE HEFSEK TAHARAH

page 8: 1. When is hefsek taharah performed?
"The earliest time at which a woman performs *hefsek taharah*..."

מעיקר הדין מותר לאשה לעשות הפסק טהרה לפני יום ה' (בתנאי שנפסק הדימום), אך אינה יכולה להתחיל במנין שבעה נקיים לפני יום ששי לתחילת ראייתה [ע' ספר האשכול (הוצאת אויערבך: ססי' מד', תורת השלמים (קצו' ס"ק יג'), חוות דעת (קצו' ביאורים ו'), סדרי טהרה (קצו' ס"ק יח' ד"ה וי"א; וס"ק לג'), שו"ת חת"ס (יו"ד ססי' קסה'; מובא בפ"ת קצו' ס"ק יד') ועוד]. ולמעשה בדרך כלל אין הנשים עושות הפסק טהרה לפני יום ה'.

page 8:
"Thus, if bleeding commences a few minutes before nightfall..."

התחלת נדות לאחר שקיעת החמה אך לפני צאת הכוכבים נחשבת עדיין ליום אחד. כן שמעתי ממו"ר הג"ר ש. ראזענבאום שליט"א. וטעם הדבר:

איתא ברמ"א (קצו' יא') "ויש שכתבו שיש להמתין עד יום א' דהיינו שלא תתחיל למנות עד יום הששי והוא יהיה יום ראשון לספירתה דחיישינן שמא תשמש ביום ראשון בין השמשות ותסבור שהוא יום ואפשר שהוא לילה. ואם תתחיל למנות מיום חמישי יהיה תוך ששה עונות לשמושה על כן יש להוסיף עוד יום א' דמעתה אי אפשר לבא לידי טעות (ת"ה סימן רמ"ה האגור בשם מהרי"ל וש"י וכן כתב מהרא"י ומהרי"ק שורש ל"ה) וכן נהגין בכל מדינות אלו ואין לשנות". ומסתבר לומר שאין צריך לחשוש בראיית בין השמשות זו שמא הוא לילה, ולהמתין עוד יום עד ימי "שבעה נקיים", דהרי כבר הוספנו יום החמישי עבור חשש זה.

וכך לדבר מצאתי בתשובת מהרש"ל (פב'; מובא בש"ך קצו' ס"ק יט'). וז"ל: "שאלה: אשה שראתה אחר ערבית ביום א' ועדיין יום הוא אם היא יכולה ללבוש נקיים ביום ה' כדרך שנוהגים הנשים וכו' או נימא מאחר שהוא אחר תפילת ערבית חשבינן כאלו ראתה ביום שלאחריו. תשובה: יראה לפי מנהג נשים שלנו שאינן לובשים נקיים עד יום ה' לראייתה ומתחילות למנות מיום ו' לראייתה אין ספיקא בדבר כי עיקר חומרת הנשים משום ראיית ביה"ש הוא שלא תהא טועה וחחשבת ליום שלפניו ושמא הוא לילה ושייך ליום שלאחריו **ואם כן מאחר שמוספת יום אחד להציל מאותו ספק א"כ אין עוד חשש בדבר בנידון דידן וזו אין צריכה רבה...**".

הרי לנו כעין סברת מו"ר הג"ר ראזענבאום שליט"א. אלא שהמהרש"ל מיירי בענין תפלת ערבית ולא של בין השמשות. אבל משמע מלשונו דלא שייך לומר "לא פלוג", אלא אפילו המחמיר בשאר מקומות אחר תפלת ערבית, כאן כיון שמוסיפים יום אחד, אין להחמיר. ולכאורה ה"ה בנידון דידן. (אע"פ שיש לחלק בין בין השמשות החמור ובין התחללה ערבית בעוד יום הקל, עכ"פ כיון שפשיטא ליה להמהרש"ל דבנשים הממתינות ה' ימים כדכתב "אין ספיקא בדבר... וזו אין צריכה רבה", משמע דפשיטא ליה למאוד דאין לומר "לא פלוג" ולכאורה ה"ה בנד"ד).

ובעזה"י מצאתי בשו"ת חשב האפוד (ח"ג עא') ממש כנ"ל. וגם בספר בדי השלחן (קצו' בה"ש ס"ק קסט') ובספר אהל שרה (מאת הגרי"י נויבירט שליט"א; ח"ב א') כתבו דראייה בבין השמשות נחשבת עדיין ליום שעבר.

ורצ"ע על מש"כ בספר שיעורי שבט הלוי (קצו' א' ט"ז א'; שם יא' ד'; ושם ש"ך יט') דמדברי הש"ך בשם מהרש"ל הנ"ל משמע דאם ראתה בבין השמשות נחשב כתחילת הלילה ולא הקילו בספק. דהרי כתבנו לעיל דמדברי מהרש"ל משמע להקל.

גם בפותח שער (טז' ג'; ע' שם שמיקל קצת לענין זמני שקיעה), ובתשובת הג"ר משה פיינשטיין ז"ל בסוף ספר הלכות נדה (מאת הג"ר שמען ד. אייזער שליט"א; ע' שם שמיקל עד ט' דקות אחר השקיעה), ובטהרת בת ישראל (ג' ד') מחמירים בבין השמשות.

page 10: 4. White underwear and bedding

"Preferably, the sheets on her bed should also be white and clean..."

בזמנינו שנשים שלנו לובשות תחתונים לבנים ונקיים גם בלילה, מעיקר הדין א"צ עוד שתציע על
מטתה סדין לבן ונקי. ורק בזמנם שישנו בלא בגדים היה הבירור על ידי הסדין. מ"מ נכון מנהגם
להציע ג"כ סדין.

ועוד נלע"ד להוסיף, דהנה בזמניהם שהיו ישנים בלא בגדים, היה די בסדין לבן, דאם יצא דם,
ממילא היה נופל על הסדין. אבל בזמנינו שלובשים בגדי לילה, חיובת ללבוש בגד תחתון לבן
הצמוד לגוף, ולא די בסדין לבן, דאל"כ הרי יפול הדם על בגד לילה, ואם הוא רק מעט לא יהיה
ניכר כלל על הסדין. או תלבש בגד לילה לבן וגם סדין לבן (ולא סגי בבגד לילה לבן דהרי שכיח
שהבגד יזוז). אך צריכה להזהר שהבגד לילה לא יהיה שקוף (דשכיח מאוד בבגדים לבנים שהם
שקופים), שלא יהיה גופה נראה, משום צניעות.

וכן הנהגות ללבוש בכל אופן בגד לילה לבן בזמן ז' נקיים (כלומר תחתונים לבנים וגם בגד לילה לבן)
צריכות להזהר שהבגד לילה לא יהיה שקוף, דאל"כ יצאו שכרן בהפסידן.

page 10: 5. Moch Dachuk (מוך דחוק) - a final check for hefsek taharah

"After a 'clean' bedikah..."

כדי שלא לסבך הענין כתבנו סתם לעשות "מוך דחוק" ולא חילקנו בין הפסק טהרה ביום ראשון
לראייתה - שאז מוך דחוק הוא חיוב, לבין הפסק טהרה מיום שני לראייתה והלאה - שאו רק
"מנהג כשר" לעשות מוך דחוק.

וכן בסעיף 2 לא כתבנו לחלק בבדיקה בשחרית בין יום ראשון לראייתה ליום שני והלאה, אלא
כתבנו סתם שבדיקת הפסק טהרה צריכה לעשות לפני שקיעת החמה, ולא כתבנו כלום ממתי
יכולה לעשות את הבדיקה.

לענין לצאת בשבת עם מוך דחוק בתוך הנרתיק, במקום שאין עירוב: ע׳ בפוסקי זמנינו [שו"ת
אגרות משה (או"ח ח"ג מז'), שו"ת אז נדברו (ח"ז מב') שו"ת באר משה (ח"א טז'), שו"ת מנחת יצחק (ח"ד כח'
אות ט'; ח"ה לז'), שו"ת ציץ אליעזר (ח"י יג'), שמירת שבת כהלכתה (יח' כ' אות פו' בשם הגרש"ז אויערבך
זצ"ל; תע"ע מש"כ ע"ז בחלק ג' הנקרא "תיקונים ומלואים"), שו"ת תשורת שי (שיט') ועוד] שדנו בזה.

page 11

"She does this by inserting a fresh *bedikah*-cloth..."

את המוך דחוק אינה צריכה לסובבו בחורים ובסדקים. אולם עצה טובה שגם במוך דחוק תסובב
כמו בבדיקה, דאם יתעורר ספק בכשרות בבדיקת "הפסק טהרה", תוכל להשתמש במוך דחוק
כבדיקה.

page 11: 6. Hefsek taharah on Shabbat, Yom Tov and Yom Kippur

ויש להזהר להכין בדי-בדיקה לפני שבת, יו"ט ויו"כ, שהרי אסור לקרוע. ובלאו הכי רצוי שיהיה
לה תמיד מספר בדי-בדיקה מוכנים.

Chapter 3: COUNTING THE "SEVEN CLEAN DAYS"

page 12: 1. The bedikot (בדיקות - examinations) - when?

"The morning *bedikah* should preferably take place after sunrise..."

ע׳ בפתוחה שער (יח' ח' במילואים) שהאריך למדברי הסדרי טהרה (קצ"י אות יט') מבואר דס"ל
דהבדיקה הוי משום ספירה וצריך להיות ביום דוקא. ובגמרא מגילה (כ׳.) איתא דספירת לילה
לא הוי ספירה. ולפי זה צריך ליזהר בבדיקת שחרית שתעשה הבדיקה בכתחילה לאחר הנץ
החמה וברדיעבד כשרה מעלות השחר. אבל לפני כן אינה בדיקה המועילה לספירה (ואם תעשה רק
בדיקה אחת בשחרית של יום ראשון, וזה יהיה עוד לפני עלות השחר, הרי אין לה בדיקת יום ראשון).

אולם מצד שני כתב הב"י (קצ"י ד"ה ומ"ש רבינו שבסה"מ) בשם סמ"ג דבשחרית תבדוק כשעומדת
ממטתה. והטעם של בדיקת שחרית כתב הב"ח (קצ"י ד"ה ובכל שבעה) "להוציאה מידי ספק שמא

ראתה בלילה", וכ"כ הסדרי טהרה (קצו' אות יד'). ולפי זה טוב לסמוך בדיקתה לקימה ממטה. לכן הזמן המובחר לבדיקת שחרית הוא סמוך לקימתה ממטה, אבל לאחר הנץ החמה.

page 12
"It is important for a woman to make a *bedikah* twice daily."

ולענין היסח הדעת, כתב בפתיחת שער (יח' כב') "...דעת המעי"ץ הובא בפת"ש (סק"ג) להחמיר וכן דעת הסד"ט (סקי"ח), אך זקני ההוראה מורין בזה כהכרעת שו"ת הצמח צדק להגה"ק מהרמ"מ ז"ל (ליובאוויטש) יו"ד (סי' קנ"ה) להקל, כמש"כ חותני הרב שליט"א בשו"ת חשה"א (ח"א סי' ק"ב) בשם הגאון מו"ה שמשון פאלאנסקי ז"ל מטעפליק שהיתה הוראתו מקובלת בירושלים ובשם הגאון מו"ה חיים ירוחם ז"ל מאלדשטאדט. וכן הקיל בשו"ת מהרש"ם (ח"ג סי' קי"ד)." עכ"ד.

page 14: 2. The bedikah (בדיקה) - *how is it done?*
"As the skin in the vagina is quite sensitive, the cloth must be soft..."

עוד טעם מובא בפוסקים, משום שקודם הכיבוס, הבד חלק ואינו מקבל כ"כ את הדם. ולשני הטעמים אינו מעכב.

page 15: 3. *White underwear and bedding*
"...and the bed linen should be clean and white."

ע' מש"כ לעיל פרק ב סעיף 4.

Chapter 4: IMMERSION IN THE MIKVEH

page 21: 5. Tevilah on Friday night or at the beginning of Yom Tov
"However, she may immerse only after nightfall on Shabbat."

ולענין אכילה בליל שבת בין חפיפה לטבילה בשעת הדחק (כגון במקום שמתפללים בעוד היום גדול, וגם אוכלים מבעוד יום) ע' שו"ת חשב האפוד (ח"ב קלח'), בדי השלחן (קצט' סעי' ו' ביאורים סד"ה תחץ), שיעורי שבט הלוי (סימן קצח' סעיף כד' אות ו' [אך ע' שם סעיף כה' אות ו']) וספר אהל שרה (ג' ו'), שאפשר להקל לאכול לפני הטבילה (אך תיזהר שלא לאכול בשר) ותנקר את השיניים היטב לפני לכתה לטבילה.

page 25: 10. After tevilah
"Bathing or showering immediately after the *mikveh* should be avoided..."

ע' ב"י (יו"ד סס' רא' ד"ה וכתב עוד המרדכי) ודרכי משה (שם אות ל') דדעת רוב ראשונים דגזרת 'הבא ראשו ורובו במים שאובים לאחר טבילה' אינו אלא לפסול לתרומה אבל לא לבעלה. וכן משמע דעת השו"ע (מדלא הביא דין זה) וכן פסק הגר"א בביאורו (סס' רא'). אך הרמ"א (רא' עה') כתב ד'יש אוסרים וכן נהגו'. וכיון שאינו אלא חומרא, מסתבר כדברי שבט הלוי (ח"ד סימן קכה') דסגי במה שבעלה נוגע בה, שבזה כבר הועילה הטבילה ולא שייך עוד למגזר 'לא אלו מטהרין אלא אלו מטהרין'. וכן אם עסקה בתוך הבית בדברים שיכולים ללכלך אותה, מותרת לרחוץ.

וכל זה דוקא אם רוצה לרחוץ ראשה ורוב גופה, אבל לרחוץ רק הגוף בלא הראש בלאו הכי מותר, דהרי גזרו רק על 'הבא ראשו ורובו במים שאובין' כדאיתא בגמרא שבת (יד').

Chapter 5: BECOMING A NIDDAH

page 28: 2. Sensation of a discharge
"A woman who feels liquid flowing from her vagina..."

בדין הרגשת זיבת דבר לח נחלקו האחרונים. הנודע ביהודה (מהדו"ק יו"ד נה') חשבה להרגשה

דאורייתא, וכן ס"ל דהמהרש"ך (מובא בשו"ת שב יעקב דלהלן). אך בשו"ת פני יהושע (ח"א יו"ד א') ושו"ת שב יעקב (ח"א סי' לט') כתבו דאינה נחשבת להרגשה כלל. וכן ס"ל דהחתם סופר (יו"ד קמה", קנג', קסז', קעא'), וכתב (יו"ד קנג' ד"ה ואע"ג) שכן קיבל ממורו הג"ר נתן אדלער ז"ל ושכן הוא מורה ובא הלכה למעשה. וכן פסק גם הסדרי טהרה (קצ' אות א'). והחוות דעת (קצ' א') כתב דזיבת דבר לח הוי הרגשה כשמרגשת זיבה מן המקור לפרוזדור דהיינו בפנים, אבל מה שמרגשת זיבת דבר לח מן הפרוזדור לחוץ לא נחשבת להרגשה. (ובהגהות מאת הג"ר ברוך פרענקיל ז"ל הקשה על הנו"ב הנ"ל דבמציאות א"א להרגיש זיבה שבתוך חלל הגוף רק כשסומך לאויר העולם).

וע' בפתוח שער (סימן ג') ושו"ת שבט הלוי (ח"ב פח'; ח"ה קב' ג'; ח"ה קיג') שהאריכו בדבר, והסכימו דהעיקר כדברי החת"ס הנ"ל.

וכתב הפתוח שער (ג' ו') דהרגשת זיבת דבר לח שבזמנינו אינו אלא ליחות חיצוני, ואינו נחשב כלל להרגשה, אלא דעכ"פ תעיין בבגדה לראות מהו הליחות. וע' בשו"ת חת"ס (יו"ד קמה') שכתב ג"כ בשאלה שנשאל דתקנה עצמה ותעיין בשעה שהכתם לח, ע' שם.

ואם לא מצאה שום הפרשה, כתבנו שתעשה בדיקה בד-הבדיקה. והטעם לזה, דהרי כיון שלא מצאה שום הפרשה, הרגשה שהרגישה ודאי לא היה זיבת דבר לח מבחוץ. אלא ע"כ או מחמת עצבנות מחשבה שהרגישה אבל באמת לא היה כלום (וכן שכיח) או שבאמת היה לה איזה הרגשה. לכן מסתבר שיש לה לבדוק א"ע. ואם רגילה בזה תבדוק עכ"פ שלש פעמים כדי לחזק א"ע במראות טהורות (ע' חכמת אדם קיג' ג', פתוח שער ג' ו', ושו"ת שבט הלוי ח"ב פח').

אולם אין להחמיר כלל בכאן כדינא דתרומת הדשן לענין פתיחת המקור (דאם לא מצאה כלום על בד-הבדיקה - טמאה), אלא כ"ז שאין מראה טמא על הבד, הרי האשה טהורה. ע' פתחי תשובה (קצ' ס"ק ד'), שו"ת שבט הלוי (ח"ה קיג' אות ו'), פותח שער (ג' טז').

"should check her underwear and..."

ע' בפתוח שער (ג' ו' ; ג' יג'-יד') ובשו"ת שבט הלוי (ח"ה קיג') ותשובת הגר"מ פיינשטיין ז"ל בסוף ספר הלכות נדה (מאת הג"ר שמעון ד. אידער שליט"א) מתי נחשב ל"מראה" ומתי ל"כתם", וצל"ע.

page 29: 3. Opening of the uterus

"In any other case, a Rabbi must be consulted..."

לא כתבנו סתם שהיא טמאה כשלא מצאה כלום (כמבואר בשו"ע קצ' א'), מכמה טעמים: 1) בימינו תופעה זו נדירה, ויכול להיות שהרגשתה אינה "פתיחת המקור" המובא בפוסקים. 2) יש יוצאים מן הכלל, ע' פתחי תשובה (קצ' ס"ק ה'-ז'). 3) הרי לעולם תוציא הבדיקה מלוכלכת מלחלוחי הגוף, ורוב נשים אינן בקיאות להחליט מה נקרא "לא מצאה כלום", ע' פתחי תשובה (קצ' ס"ק ו').

page 29: 4. Staining (ketem - כתם)

"...found on a completely colored background..."

ע' באחרונים דיש אם נמצא חלק על צבע וחלק על לבן. וכדי שלא לסבך את הענין כתבתי להקל רק כשנמצא כולו על מקום צבע. ואם רק חלק מהכתם על מקום צבע, נכלל במה שכתבנו "בכל שאר מקרים יש לשאול את הרב".

page 29:

"Several separate stains, each smaller than the size shown below..."

השו"ע בסימן קצ' סעיף ו' כתב "הא דבעינן שיעורא בין בכתם הנמצא על חלוקה בין בכתם הנמצא על בשרה וי"א שלא אמרו אלא בכתם הנמצא על חלוקה אבל כתם הנמצא על בשרה בלבד במקומות שחוששין להם אין לו שיעור". אולם בשו"ע שם בסעיף ח' סתם כדברי האומר דגם בבשרה צריך שיעור כגריס, אלא דבכתמים קטנים שעל בשרה י"א שמצרפים אותם משא"כ בכתם שעל בגד. הש"ך פסק להחמיר בכתם שעל בשרה שא"צ שיעור. אבל הב"ח, תורת השלמים והסדרי טהרה פסקו להקל, דגם על בשרה יש דין כתם. ומשמע מהספרים של קיצור הלכות נדה, דסוגיין דעלמא להקל.

"After a gynecological examination of the uterus..."

ע' פתחי תשובה (קצד' אות ד') בענין "אי אפשר לפתיחת הקבר בלא דם". ומסקנת האחרונים להחמיר גם בפתיחת הרחם מבחוץ. אולם על ידי האצבע לחוד א"א לפתוח את פי הרחם. וע' בשו"ת חשב האפוד (ח"ב ז' ד"ה ויש עוד לדעת) שכתב "ויש עוד לדעת שהאם יש לה שתי פיות (והזכיר דבר זה הבית יצחק יו"ד ח"ב סי' י"ד) פה אחד פנימי שהוא סוגר את האם, ולפני אותו הפה יש כמו פרוזדור קטן כדמות צואר אשר הרופאים קוראים אותו צואר האם, ובתחלת אותו צואר יש גם כן כמו פה. ואמנם מה שאמרו אי אפשר לפתיחת הקבר בלי דם, הכוונה על פה הפנימי שהוא את פי האם ממש, שהוא סגור ומסוגר ואינו ופתיחתו אינו דבר קל. משא"כ הפה החיצון שהוא פי צואר האם עליו אינו שייך לומר שאי אפשר לפתיחתו בלא דם...".

אולם בשיעורי שבט הלוי (קפח' אות ד' ד"ה ולהלכה) כתב "ובתשובות הב"ח החדשות (סל"ה) פליגי הג"ר פיינבוש והב"ח הסמ"ע מהו פתיחת הקבר, דברחם יש כניסה מהרחם לצואר וגם מבית החיצון (נרתיק) לצואר, וי"א דפה"ק הוא רק בפתח הפנימי, אך ההוראה באחרונים להחמיר בפתח צואר הרחם (ועיין מש"כ בסימן קצ"ו ס"ו אות ח')".

ובעניות דעתי לא זכיתי להבין דברי השיעורי שבט הלוי. דבתשובות הב"ח החדשות (סימן לד', לה') לא נחלקו בענין "אי אפשר לפתיחת הקבר בלא דם", אלא בענין מתי נעשית האשה נדה, ברגע שיצא שיצא דם מפתח הפנימי או רק משיצא דם מפתח החיצון, ולמה אין האשה חייבת לבדוק עד פתח הפנימי. ע' שם היטב. ברם לענין דין של "אי אפשר לפתיחת הקבר בלא דם", לענ"ד מוכרח דכ"ע מודה דהיינו הפתח הפנימי. דהרי כתבו שם לפרש דברי הרמב"ם (איסורי ביאה ה' ב'-ד') דבשעת גמר ביאה נכנס האבר קצת לפנים מפתח החיצון. ואת"ל ד"פתיחת הקבר" ר"ל פתיחת פתח החיצון, הרי בכל גמר ביאה נפתח הפתח? אלא ע"כ צ"ל דאפילו להג"ר פיינבוש (שס"ל דהאשה טמאה רק כשיצא הדם מפתח החיצון) מה שנאמר דא"א לפתיחת הקבר בלא דם, כוונתו לפתח הפנימי. כלומר, א"א לפתוח את פתח הפנימי בלי שיצא דם ויזוב חוץ לפתח החיצון, אבל פתח החיצון אפשר לפתחו גם בלי דימוים. (אולם למ"ד דוקא פתיחת הקבר מבפנים גורם לדימוים אבל לא פתיחת הקבר מבחוץ, יש מקום לומר דס"ל דגם פתח החיצון א"א לפתוח בלי דימום אבל לפי שיטה זו ממילא אין בעיא בבדיקת הרופא, דהרי ס"ל דפתיחת הקבר מבחוץ אינו מטמאה).

לפי כל הנ"ל היה נראה להקל שלא להצטריך כלל בדיקה בבד-הבדיקה לאחר בדיקת הרופא באצבעו לחוד. אולם ע' בשו"ת מנחת יצחק (ח"ב פד'), שו"ת באר משה (ח"ג קמז'), שו"ת דברי משה (נג'), פותח שער (ו' ח'), שיעורי שבט הלוי (קפח' אות ד' ד"ה ובבדיקת הרופאים), שכולם כתבו שלכתחילה תבדוק האשה אב"א, ע' שם. אך שמעתי ממקורות נאמנים שמרן פדווא שליט"א אב"ד דקה"ה לונדון פוסק שלא לעשות בדיקה וכן שמעתי מכמה מורי הוראה. (ובמעוברת אפשר גם המחמירים לכתחילה מודים להקל, כי דעת הרופאים שטוב להם למעט בבדיקות. וכן בשאר מקום הצורך).

"If the inner cervix was opened, she must consult a Rabbi..."

אם נפתח פי המקור בכלי שעב יותר ממה שנקרא "דק שבדקין", היא טמאה גם אם הבדיקה יצא טהורה. ואם לא נפתח המקור (או רק ב"דק שבדקין"), הרי היא טהורה וא"צ בדיקה. אולם מכיון שבעניינים אלה יש בדרך כלל הרבה ספיקות, צירופים וכו', חייבת לשאול את הרב.

Chapter 6: SEPARATION DURING THE TIME OF NIDDAH

"The Torah states: 'Do not come close to a woman who is ritually unclean...'"

ואפילו למ"ד דחיבוק ונישוק אינו אלא מדרבנן וכן שאר קריבות שאינם של חיבה שאסרו חז"ל, עכ"פ רמז התורה לרבותינו ז"ל לאוסרו מדרבנן. וע' ריטב"א (ר"ה טז. ד"ה תניא) לפירוש "אסמכתא", שהעיר הקב"ה שראוי לעשות כן אלא שלא קבעו חובה ומסרו לחכמים. וע' גם בגור אריה (פרשת יתרו יט' טו').

וכן איתא באבות דר' נתן (פ"ב) המובא בשו"ע (קצה' א'), וע' בב"י (קצה' ד"ה ומ"ש ולא מתשמיש). חז"ל האבות דר' נתן: "ואל אשה בנדת טומאתה לא תקרב יכול יחבקנה וינשקנה

וידבר עמה דברים בטלים ת"ל לא תקרב. יכול ישן עמה בבגדיה על המטה ת"ל לא תקרב...", ע'
שם. וכן ע' גמרא שבת (יג.\.):.

page 32: 1. Physical contact and intimacy
"A husband and wife must not sit together on a movable item..."

דין ישיבה על ספסל אחד באוטו (מכונית), **אוטובוס וכדומה**: ע' היטב בתרומת הדשן (רנא')
ורמ"א (קצה' ה'). וע' בפוסקי זמנינו [שו"ת אג"מ (יו"ד ח"א סס"י צב'; ח"ב סס"י עז'), שו"ת באר משה (ח"א
נ' אות טו'; ח"ב סד' אות ר'; ח"ג קלג'), שו"ת שבט הלוי (ח"ו קכ"ט ט'), פותח שער (טו' מב'), שו"ת משנה
הלכות (ח"ה קמד'), טהרת בת ישראל (ב' יא'; ומכתב החז"א שם) ועוד].

page 32:
"...or a sizeable object is placed between them..."

לשון הרמ"א (קצה' ה') "ויש מתירים כשאדם אחר מפסיק ויושב ביניהם", ומקורו בספר האגודה
(סוף פרק התינוקת) וז"ל "שיפסיק אדם אחר ביניהם או תיבה או שום דבר" ומביאו הב"י (קצה'
ד"ה וכתוב עוד) בזה הלשון.

page 33:
"A ride solely for pleasure..."

ע' היטב במרדכי (שבת פרק א' אות רלח'), בספר האגודה (סוף נדה אות מג'), בשו"ת תרומת
הדשן (רנא'), בבית יוסף (קצה' ד"ה וכתוב עוד בתרומות הדשן), בדרכי משה (קצה' אות ה')
וברמ"א (קצה' ה'). הנה מדברי הפוסקים הנ"ל משמע להדיא דדין עגלה וספינה בא לו מדינא של
ספסל המתנדנדת, דהיינו שאפשר יש לדמות נסיעה בעגלה ובספינה דרך טיול לספסל המתנדנדת.
וכן מורה לשון הרמ"א שכתב "ואסור לישב על ספסל... וכן לא ילך עם אשתו בעגלה אחת או
בספינה אחת אם הולך רק דרך טיול...".

ולפי זה מה שהקל הרמ"א בדברי האגודה לישב על ספסל המתנדנדת כשאדם אחר מפסיק ויושב
ביניהם (ולכאורה ה"ה כשחפץ מונח ביניהם, כמבואר באגודה הנ"ל) כל שכן בנסיעה בעגלה אחת או
ספינה אחת דרך טיול, מותר כשאדם או חפץ מפסיק. וכן כתב בפירוש בחכמת אדם (קטז' ה')
"ואם אדם מפסיק ביניהם לא גרע מספסל המתנדנדת דמותר", ע' שם.
וע' בדרכי תשובה (קצה' אות ל'; בשם שו"ת שערי צדק דלא כנ"ל [אך גם הדרכי תשובה חולק עליו]) ובבדי
השלחן (קצה' ס"ק צג' וביאורים שם). אך כנ"ל נראה ברור. ובפרט שהוראה זו של נסיעה בעגלה ובספינה הוא
רק ספק של חומרא, שהרי כתב התה"ד דדין ספסל המתנדנדת היא חומרא, ובנסיעה בעגלה 'לא בריראא
להתיר' דאפשר דומה לחומרת ספסל המתנדנדת. והב"י כתב דהספרדים לא נוהגים כלל כחומרת ספסל
העגלה ולכן לא הביא דין זה כלל בספרו שו"ע [וכ"כ הברכי יוסף (קצה' רמ"א ה') שהספרדים לא נוהגים
בחומרא זו כלל].

ונראה לענ"ד דבנסיעה בעגלה ובספינה לטיול, לא רק אם בעל ואשתו יושבים בספסל אחת צריך
אדם או חפץ להפסיק ביניהם, אלא גם אם בעל ואשתו יושבים אחד ממול השני צריך להפסיק -
משום שכל העגלה והספינה נחשבת לספסל המתנדנדת. דהרי התרומת הדשן לא רצה להתיר
אפילו באופן שהוא יושב לפנים והיא לאחור [ע' לשון השאלה בתה"ד הנ"ל. וידוע מש"כ הש"ך (יו"ד
קצו' ס"ק כ') וט"ז (יו"ד שכח' ס"ק ב') ובית שמואל (אה"ע קל' ס"ק כ') ועוד, שבעל תה"ד הוא עצמו סידר
שאלותיו]. הרי לך שעצם הנדנוד של העגלה או ספינה נחשב לספסל המתנדנד, ולא דוקא
כשיושבים על ספסל אחד של העגלה. ומה שאנו מקילים כדברי האגודה שמתיר כשאדם יושב
ביניהם, היינו דגם בעגלה או ספינה נחשב אדם לישב ביניהם, אפילו אם בעל ואשתו יושבים על
ספסלים נפרדים, כי כל העגלה וספינה נחשבין לספסל אחד [דלא כטהרת בת ישראל (ב' יא')].
ולכאורה מסתבר שהאדם צריך להיות ביניהם, ולא סגי בזה שאדם אחר ג"כ על הספינה, דהרי גם
בספסל ארוך לא התיר האגודה אלא ביושב ביניהם ולא סגי כשאדם אחר יושב מן הצד על
הספסל.

ולענין נסיעה דרך טיול **באוטו** (מכונית), ע' בדברי הפוסקים לעיל (בד"ה דין ישיבה על ספסל אחד
באוטו).

page 33:

"The husband may not gaze at those parts of his wife's body which are usually covered."

דין שמיעת קול זמר של אשתו נדה: הפתחי תשובה (קצה' ס"ק י') נשאר בצ"ע. וע' בתועפות ראם על ספר יראים (סימן כו' אות קל') מה שהקשה על דברי הפתחי תשובה, ודעתו להתיר. וכן פסק בשו"ת יביע אומר (ח"ד יו"ד טו') ובספרו טהרת הבית (ח"ב סימן יב' סעיף כט'). אך מסקנת רוב האחרונים להחמיר ולחם ושמלה (קצה' ס"ק כ') וכן בספרו קשו"ע (קנג' י'), דרכי תשובה (קצה' אות לה'), ערוך השלחן (קצה' כג'), שו"ת אג"מ (יו"ד ח"ב עה'); כתב "מהראוי להחמיר", ע' שם), פותח שער (טו' מוי'), שיעורי שבט הלוי (קצה' ו' אות ב'; וע' שו"ת שבט הלוי ח"ו קכט' אות יב') ועוד). וכן סוגיין דעלמא להחמיר.

וע"ע בבן איש חי (שנה שניה פרשת צו אות כה').

page 33: 2. In the bedroom

"They may not put clean bedding on each other's bed..."

זה לשון השו"ע (קצה' יא'): "אסורה להציע מטתו בפניו וו'רוכא פריסת סדינים והמכסה שהוא דרך חבה אבל הצעת הכרים והכסתות שהוא טורח ואינו דרך חבה שרי ושלא בפניו הכל מותר אפילו הוא יודע שהיא מצעת אותם".

וע' בפוסקי זמנינו (שיעורי שבט הלוי קצה' יא' אות ב'; פותח שער טו' לד'; ועוד) דאיסור הצעת המטה, היינו כשהוא הכנת המטה לשינה, שדבר זה נחשב למעשה של חיבה אולם סידור המטות כדי שהחדר יראה מסודר, אין בו איסור.

ועוד כתב בשיעורי שבט הלוי (קצה' יא' אות ד') "ויש להסתפק בכרים וכסתות בזה"ז שאינם כבדים כ"כ דשמא יש לאסור גם בהם ולא רק בסדינים, דכשהם קלים אינו מעשה עבדות, וי"א דזו כוונת הש"ך שציין לאה"ע דהיינו שהוא ענין של חיבה ולא כמחבר שמיקל וכתב דהוא טורח, ולכן בכרים וכסתות קלים שהוא בקרן מגון יש להחמיר, דאינו טירחא ומעשה עבדות", וע"ע בפרי דעה (שפתי לוי קצה' אות טו'). וצל"ע.

Chapter 7: THE EXPECTED TIME OF THE NEXT PERIOD

page 37: 2. Separation and bedikah on the expected date of the next period

"A woman may find it useful to wear white underwear during that time."

כ"כ בשו"ת אגרות משה (יו"ד ח"ג מח'). וכן מסתבר, ובפרט לאלו המקילים לבדוק רק פעם אחת.

page 40. The irregular cycle

"It is recommended that... a woman should also check on these 'unsafe days'..."

אע"פ שמצד הדין לא חששנו לפירוש הנוב"י בדברי הרמ"י (קפד' ב') באשה שמשנית וסתה, ולא כדעת הרא"ש ורמב"ם בשו"ע (קפו' ב'), מ"מ כדאי עכ"פ לודא לפני התשמיש שהאשה טהורה. וכ"פ בשו"ת אג"מ (יו"ד ח"ב מח') ופותח שער (כד' ח'-י').

אולם די בזה בקינוח וא"צ בדיקת חורין וסדקין, דהיינו שתשהה העד על על עצמה איזה זמן קצר בשעה שאינה שוכבת אפרקיד, ע' חוו"ד (קפו') ופותח שער (כד' י').

וע' בשיעורי שבט הלוי (קפו' ב' אות יב' ד"ה ולהלכה).

page 42. The regular cycle

"In addition to the regular cycles mentioned above..."

דין וסת מחמת אונס ע' בשו"ע (קפט' יז', יח'). **דין וסת על ידי אכילת דברים חריפים** ע' ברמ"א (קפט' כג').

page 42: 6. Breaking a regular cycle

"In order for an established regular cycle to be broken... without any flow of blood..."

ואם ראתה לפני זמן וסתה, וראיתה נמשכה לזמן וסת הקבוע, לא נעקר על ידי זה, ע' בחוו"ד

(קפד' ביאורים ד'), ורשו"ע הרב (קפט' אות לח').

דין וסת קבוע לאחר ימי ההריון וההנקה, ע' לקמן סעיף 8.

page 43: 7. Premenstrual physical symptoms
"If this pattern repeats itself three consecutive times, she has established a regular cycle."

ולענין אם אשה יש לה וסת הגוף צריכה לחוש לעונה בינונית או לא, והאם יש נ"מ לענין זה בין וסת הגוף לחוד לבין וסת הגוף המורכב בימים: ע' רמב"ן (הל' נדה פ"ד), רשב"א (תורת הבית הארוך בית ז' שער ג'), ב"י (סס' קפד') ורשו"ע (קפד' יב'), ש"ך (קפד' ס"ק לב'), תורת השלמים (קפד' אות כד'), ס"ט (סס' קפד'), חוו"ד (קפד' ביאורים טו') ורשו"ע הרב (קפד' אות מה'). ובמקום אחר הארכתי, ואכ"מ.

page 44: 8. During pregnancy and breastfeeding
"When she has ceased breastfeeding, she must once again..."

ע' שו"ע (קפט' לד') וש"ך (קפט' ס"ק עה').

ודוקא לוסתה הקבוע חוזרת לחוש אבל לא לוסתה שאינו קבוע, פתחי תשובה (קפט' ס"ק לב') בשם נו"ב.

ע' בפוסקי זמנינו [שו"ת אג"מ (יו"ד ח"ג נב'), שו"ת שבט הלוי (ח"ג קיד'; ח"ד צט'; ח"ד קיא' א') ועוד. ולענין דעת החז"א ע' ההלכה במשפחה (פ"ט מקורות אות 19) וחוט השני (קפט' לג' אות יח')] שדנו האם הדין של מסולקת דמים לאחר ג' חדשים מתחילת עיבורה עד כד' חדש אחר הלידה נשתנה בזמנינו. ולמעשה אין כ"ב נ"מ.

א) לענין ג"ח ראשונים: אם היה לה וסת שאינו קבוע, בל"ה נעקר בפ"א שלא ראתה וא"צ לחוש שוב. (ואם יש לה וסת בתחלת ימי עיבורה, הא בל"ה צריכה לחוש לה כוסת שאינו קבוע כדאיתא בשו"ע קפט' לג'.) וכן אם היה לה וסת קבוע להפלגות, מפעם ראשונה שאין לה וסת הרי לא שייך לחוש ע"פ לוסת הפלגה. אלא הנ"מ הוא כשיש לה וסת קבוע לימי החודש. וכן לענין לקבוע וסת חדש.

ב) לאחר ההנקה עוד לפני עבור כד' חדשים: לוסת שאינו קבוע בל"ה צריכה לחוש (שו"ע קפט' לג'). והנ"מ רק לענין לחוש לוסת קבוע שהיה לה (ולכמה פוסקים נ"מ לענין ע"ב) וכן לקבוע וסת חדש.

ומסתבר לחוש - עכ"פ לחומרא - דהיינו לחוש לאחר ההנקה לוסתה הקבוע הקורם. וכן אם קובעת וסת חדש בימים אלו, יש לחוש לזה (ובזה אפשר לצדד לומר דקבע אפילו להקל).

Chapter 8: THE BRIDE

page 46: 1. Before the wedding - general rules
"Every bride... must make a *hefsek taharah*...."

בסתם נשים, שיש להם וסת, ההפסק טהרה מעיקר הדין. אולם בנשים שהם בגיל המעבר (זקנה שאין לה עוד אורח נשים) ושאר מסולקות דמים, שאין לחוש אלא לדם חימוד, מעיקר הדין אינם צריכות הפסק טהרה, אלא רק ספירת ז' נקיים. אבל כבר נהגו, שכל הכלות עושות הפסק טהרה. פרטים ע' בשו"ע (קצב') ונושא כליו (שם).

page 47: 3. After the wedding - general rules
"All the laws of *niddah* apply..."

עוד נ"מ יש, כמש"כ בשו"ע (קצז') "ונהגו עמה בכל דיני נדה לענין הרחקה; אלא שנדה גמורה אסור לו לישן על מטתו אפילו כשאינה במטה, וזו מותר לו לישן באותה מטה, לאחר שעמדה מאצלו, ואפילו בסדין שהדם שהדם עליו."

page 47.

"If the woman experiences pain during the second intercourse..."

ע' ערוך השלחן (קצג' יא'), טהרת בת ישראל (טו' ח'), ושו"ת מנחת יצחק (ח"ה סא'). [וע"ש שו"ת מנחת יצחק שהקל מטעם ספק ספיקא (ס"ס בראורייתא וספק א' דרבנן). ובמקום אחר הארכתי להוכיח שמציאה שניה ואילך לא גזרו חז"ל לטמא את דם בתולים עצמם, אלא גזרו שאם מצא דם אסור לתלות בדם בתולים (כתלייה בדם שאר מכות). ולפי זה, כל זמן שלא ראתה דם שיצא, הרי האשה טהורה - דאין אנו צריכים לדין 'תליה במכה', ולא מצינו חיוב בדיקה לחפש דם. ואכמ"ל.]

page 48: 4. After the wedding - special rules

"...a woman with an irregular cycle... on her 'unsafe days'..."

כתב בהגהות חתם סופר (קפו' ב') "וזאת לדעת דהני נשי דידן דרובן יש להן וסת עד זמן ידוע ואח"כ אין להן קביעות כנון דלא חזיא בפחות מכ' יום ואחר כך אין לה קביעות אז אינו מועיל במה שבדקה ג"פ בתוך העשרים יום אלא צריכה לבדוק ג"פ בימים שאחר עשרים יום שאז דינה כמי שאין לה וסת ואותה הבדיקה מצאיאתה מספק ולא זולת זה כלל ועי' מ"ש לקמן בסק"ד אי"ה". וע' נוד"ב (יו"ד מהדו"ק סי' סא' ומהדו"ת סי' צד' ד"ה ודע). ובשיעורי שבט הלוי (קפו' ב' אות ד') הוסיף "וכן יש לנהוג לכתחילה, אך בדיעבד מהני". וע"ע בספר מראה כהן (עמוד רח') בירור מאת הרה"ג ר' משה שאול קליין שליט"א.

THE LAWS OF LIGHTING CANDLES FOR SHABBAT AND YOM TOV

page 57: 2. How many candles does one light?

"It is customary to light at least two candles."

אשה ששכחה פעם אחת להדליק את הנרות של שבת, תדליק מכאן ולהבא נר נוסף כמבואר ברמ"א (רסג' א'). ובנאנסה אינה צריכה (מ"ב שם ס"ק ז').

ואם שכחה ביו"ט, דעת שו"ת קנין תורה בהלכה (פז') וספר מבית הלוי (ניסן עמוד סז'; בשם הגר"ש ואוזר שליט"א) דא"צ להוסיף, אולם דעת שו"ת משנה הלכות (ח"ז לה'; ח"י נג', ושו"ת באר משה (ח"ה קא'), ושו"ת אז נדברו (ח"ג ה') דאין לחלק בין יו"ט לשבת צריכה להוסיף גם ביו"ט. **וע"ע שם לענין יו"ט שני של גליות.**

ואם היא או בעלה **הדליקו אור חשמל בבית** (לכבוד שבת): ע' שו"ת מלמד להועיל (או"ח מו'), שו"ת שבט הלוי (ח"ה לג'), ושו"ת ציץ אליעזר (חלק כא' יא').

THE LAWS OF SEPARATING CHALLAH FROM DOUGH

page 65: 1. Who takes challah?

"...she may ask someone else (not a child) to take *challah* on her behalf."

ולעניין קטן וקטנה שהגיעו לעונת נדרים: בשו"ע (יו"ד שכו' א') מבואר דדין חלה כדין תרומה. וע' הלכות תרומה שו"ע (יו"ד שלא' לג') וביאור הגר"א (שם). וע"ע תשובות הרמב"ם פאר הדור (עב') שכתב "קטן שהגיע לעונת נדרים ולא הביא שתי שערות אם תרם תרומתו תרומה ולכתחילה אינו יכול לתרום עד שיביא שתי שערות".

וע"ע באחרונים שדנו, האם לשיטת השו"ע (שמתיר לקטן שהגיע לעונת נדרים להפריש) מותר גם להפריש משל עיסת אחרים או אמרינן דאין שליחות לקטן.

page 67: 5. Combination of several doughs (צירוף)

"This is done by placing all the doughs or cakes in one container..."

ע' רמ"א (יו"ד שכה' א') ומפרשים שם, דבסל אינו צריך לכסות מלמעלה כל זמן שכל העיסות בתוך הכלי. אולם אם עיסה אחת בולטת לגמרי מעל לכלי, צריך לכסות אותן במפה או בכלי. ע' שם, ובביאור הלכה (תנו' א' ד"ה שיתן ודה"ה והסל).